DR. DRE

Recent Titles in Greenwood Biographies

DR. DRE

A Biography

John Borgmeyer and Holly Lang

GREENWOOD BIOGRAPHIES

GREENWOOD PRESS
WESTPORT, CONNECTICUT • LONDON

Library of Congress Cataloging-in-Publication Data

Borgmeyer, John.
    Dr. Dre : a biography / by John Borgmeyer and Holly Lang.
        p. cm.—(Greenwood biographies)
    Includes bibliographical references and index.
    ISBN 0–313–33826–4 (alk. paper)
1. Dr. Dre, 1965– 2. Rap musicians—United States—Biography.   I. Lang, Holly.
II. Title.
    ML420.D78B67   2007
    782.421649092—dc22
    [B]   2006031300

British Library Cataloguing in Publication Data is available.

Library of Congress Catalog Card Number: 2006031300

ISBN: 0–313–33826–4
ISSN: 1540–4900

First published in 2007

Greenwood Press, 88 Post Road West, Westport, CT 06881
An imprint of Greenwood Publishing Group, Inc.
www.greenwood.com

Printed in the United States of America

The paper used in this book complies with the
Permanent Paper Standard issued by the National
Information Standards Organization (Z39.48–1984).

10 9 8 7 6 5 4 3 2 1

CONTENTS

Photo essay follows page 62

SERIES FOREWORD

In response to high school and public library needs, Greenwood developed this distinguished series of full-length biographies specifically for student use. Prepared by field experts and professionals, these engaging biographies are tailored for high school students who need challenging yet accessible biographies. Ideal for secondary school assignments, the length, format and subject areas are designed to meet educators' requirements and students' interests.

Greenwood offers an extensive selection of biographies spanning all curriculum-related subject areas, including social studies, the sciences, literature and the arts, and history and politics, as well as popular culture, covering public figures and famous personalities from all time periods and backgrounds, both historic and contemporary, who have made an impact on American or world culture. Greenwood biographies were chosen based on comprehensive feedback from librarians and educators. Consideration was given to both curriculum relevance and inherent interest. The result is an intriguing mix of the well-known and the unexpected, the saints and sinners from long-ago history and contemporary pop culture. Readers will find a wide array of subject choices from fascinating crime figures like Al Capone to inspiring pioneers like Margaret Mead, from the greatest minds of our time like Stephen Hawking to the most amazing success stories of our day, like that of J.K. Rowling.

Although the emphasis is on fact, not glorification, the books are meant to be fun to read. Each volume provides in-depth information about the subject's life from birth through childhood, the teen years, and adulthood. A thorough account relates family background and education, traces personal and professional influences, and explores struggles, accomplishments, and contributions. A timeline highlights the most significant life events against a historical perspective. Bibliographies supplement the reference value of each volume.

INTRODUCTION

Andre "Dr. Dre" Young is one of the most influential artists in popular music. As a member of the controversial hip-hop group N.W.A. and, later, as a solo rapper and producer, Dr. Dre was the main creative force behind a new style of music that in the early 1990s would come to be known as "gangsta" rap, a subgenre of hip-hop, the main feature of which is a lyrical emphasis on the lifestyle of inner-city gang members.

From its inception, gangsta rap provoked heated response. The first true gangsta album, N.W.A.'s *Straight Outta Compton*, went gold in 1989, indicating that hard-core rap had "crossed over" into the mainstream pop market. The success came despite the fact that MTV and most radio stations would not play N.W.A.'s graphic content. Yet mainstream media outlets would soon embrace gangsta as the genre's popularity skyrocketed—driven by Dr. Dre and his two most significant protégés, Snoop Doggy Dogg and Eminem. By 1997, Dre's record label, Death Row, had released nine multiplatinum gangsta rap albums.

Dre's music is intense and aggressive, punctuated with graphic (and often funny) storytelling. Given the tried-and-true music industry formula of marketing controversial new artists to rebellious teens, it is perhaps not hard to understand gangsta's impressive sales. As gangsta rap grew, however, so did the criticism.

Gangsta's critics protested the genre's celebration of degeneracy, violence, alcoholism, and drug abuse. At the height of Death Row's popularity, the content of gangsta rap became a subject of debate in the 1996 presidential election, as high-ranking officials called on Time Warner to stop distributing Death Row records. Some of these attempts at censorship were based on fear and ignorance of gangsta rap, but the critics also had a point—gang activity proliferated across America in the 1990s, prompting questions about the relationship between art and life.

The biography of Dr. Dre is a story about how fantasy and reality influence each other in American culture. As an artist, Dre created gangsta rap by blending the sounds of 1970s funk and soul with the intense beats and gritty lyrics born from the gang-plagued streets of South Central Los Angeles. The story of Dr. Dre's rise to fame parallels the rise of hip-hop as one of the most dominant cultural forces in America. The tragic tale of Death Row Records, which culminates in the high-profile murders of rap artists Tupac Shakur and the Notorious B.I.G., is a lesson in what can go wrong when people in the rap business believe their own "gangsta" hype. Dre's ability to survive in the rough-and-tumble rap industry is a testament to the power of artistic vision and the payoff of sheer persistence.

Dr. Dre's life story will be worthwhile reading for anyone interested in music, culture, censorship, race, and the entertainment business in modern America. More than a few critics have dismissed Dre as just another foul-mouthed rapper corrupting young listeners, but simply criticizing gangsta artists doesn't help understand the gangsta phenomenon. For better or worse, the continuing popularity of gangsta rap is an important story about America, one that must be heard by anyone interested in the future of our society.

TIMELINE

1965:   Andre Young is born in Compton, California, on February 18.

1982:   Young joins the World Class Wreckin' Cru and adopts the name Dr. Dre.

1986:   Dre forms N.W.A. with Eazy-E and Ice Cube.

1988:   N.W.A. releases its debut, *Straight Outta Compton*.

1990:   N.W.A. releases *100 Miles and Runnin'*.

1991:   N.W.A. releases *Efil4zaggin'*, and it hits number 1 on the *Billboard* album charts.

1992:   Dre forms Death Row Records with Suge Knight. *The Chronic* is released in December. The album is continually referred to as one of the top albums of the 1990s, and it firmly established the West Coast style that made many artists, including Snoop Doggy Dogg, famous. Videos for its singles received widespread play on MTV and BET, solidifying Dre's prominence in hip-hop production.

1993:   Dre produces and releases Snoop Doggy Dogg's *Doggystyle*. The album is the first debut release to enter the *Billboard* charts at number 1. It went on to sell more than five million copies, further establishing Death Row Records as a major player in the music industry.

1994:   Dre wins several industry awards, including a Grammy Award for Best Rap Solo Performance and the Source

Awards for Artist of the Year, Album of the Year, and Producer of the Year.

1995:   Dre spends 180 days in a halfway house after an arrest and conviction. He later cites this stay as the reason for his eventually leaving Death Row Records.

1996:   Dre and Tupac Shakur release their collaboration "California Love," a number 1 single that turns out to be one of Dre's last sessions in the Death Row studios. He soon leaves the label, forms Aftermath Entertainment, and releases *Dr. Dre Presents ... The Aftermath*, which debuted to lackluster sales and widespread criticism.

1997:   Dre produces much of Nas' group The Firm's *The Firm: The Album* to poor sales, despite high critical acclaim. The group almost immediately disbanded. Aftermath artist King Tee also left the label that year after a Dre-produced album also performed poorly.

1998:   Dre signs Eminem to Aftermath; Eminem would eventually go on to be one of the highest-grossing rappers of all time.

1999:   Dre produces Eminem's breakthrough album *The Slim Shady LP*. He also releases *Chronic 2001*. Both albums sold well and received widespread accolades, giving Dre back his familiar foothold on the hip-hop industry.

2000:   Dre produces Eminem's *The Marshall Mathers* LP, which spent eight weeks at the top of the *Billboard* charts, and earned Dre a Grammy as Producer of the Year.

2001:   Dre starred in *The Wash*, a comedy set at a neighborhood car wash that also starred Snoop Doggy Dogg. Dre also recorded a single, "Bad Intentions," for the movie soundtrack.

2002:   Dre produces Eminem's *The Eminem Show*, which went platinum eight times over. The album's first single, "Without Me," features Dre both in the song and in the video, which was nominated for a number of awards.

2003:   Dre, along with Eminem, produces 50 Cent's *Get Rich or Die Tryin'*. The album and its hit single "In da Club" become the first such pair to both rank number 1 for the year on the *Billboard* charts since 1994.

2004:   Dre signs The Game to his Aftermath label, further
               boosting the artist roster, which now includes Eve,
               Busta Rhymes, and Stat Quo.

2005:   Dre releases four top-selling albums: The Game's
               The Documentary, 50 Cent's *Get Rich or Die Tryin'*
               soundtrack, 50 Cent's *The Massacre*, and Eminem's
               Curtain Call: The Hits.

Chapter 1

NUTHIN' BUT A "G" THANG

"Nuthin' but a 'G' thang": this line forms a memorable chorus from Dre's gangsta rap masterpiece, *The Chronic*. What is a "'G' thang"? The song doesn't say exactly, but Dre's music describes an attitude, a style, and a language that collectively have become known as "gangsta." Like a James Dean for the 1990s, Dre's gangsta is cool, detached, and fearless, the epitome of a rebel without a cause. Alluring, threatening, half-joking, and sometimes dead serious, Dre's gangsta rap has become one of the loudest voices for young people in America. Thanks to Dre, it seems like everybody wants to be a "G."

PAGING DR. DRE

Dr. Dre was no gang member. In 1989, Andre "Dr. Dre" Young was an up-and-coming hip-hop producer in Los Angeles. A reporter for *The Los Angeles Times* found him in what would become a familiar pose for the then 24-year-old artist: sitting in a deli in west Los Angeles, in a jacket, warm-up pants, and his trademark black baseball cap bearing the logo of the Los Angeles Raiders football team, his attempts to dig into a ham-and-cheese omelet thwarted by the nonstop beeping of his pager.

"Calling Dr. Dre. Calling Dr. Dre. Calling Dr. Dre," he droned mockingly. Dre had just burst onto the music scene and already had produced two million-selling albums. Dre couldn't carry a tune or play an instrument, but his presence in a recording studio virtually ensured that the record that emerged would hit the charts. His career had just begun, and already his work was drawing comparisons to some of the greatest producers in the history of American pop music.

That's why his beeper kept beeping. "Yo! Make it quick," Dre snapped into his mobile phone. Record executives, journalists, competing produc- ers, and music fans all wanted to know: What is it about Dre? How does he explain his Midas touch, his mysterious ability to go into the studio with almost any artist and come out with great music? Could Dre please explain how he does it?

According to the interviewer, the question made Dre frown and puzzle, as if he'd just been asked to explain nuclear physics.

"I don't know what I do, I just do it," he said. "I don't know how to explain it, because I learned how to be a producer through trial and error. It's instinct. It's feel. It's knowing what's happening on the street…. A lot of it is very spontaneous" (Hunt, 1989, p. 76).

At that moment, Dre's best work was yet to come. Still, even in the early stages of his career, people in the music industry could sense his spe- cial feel. Dre had a talent for capturing the spirit of his times and turning it into music. He was well versed in the street culture of young African Americans, and he also knew well the long tradition of African American music that had come before him. Combining those two things together, Dre constructed musical stories that grabbed the American imagination. His greatest gift, he said, was his ear.

"I have a good ear for what's authentic, for what people will like. For street rap, it has to sound real, like the kids were overhearing somebody talk on the street. A lot of rap is phony—talking about stuff people don't care about and talking about it in a way that doesn't sound real. Our stuff is hip because it's real. The fans can tell right away" (Hunt, 1989, p. 76).

WELCOME TO THE "G" THANG

In 1988, Dre introduced the world to "real" hard-core rap when he and the Los Angeles rap group N.W.A. stormed onto the music scene with their debut album, *Straight Outta Compton*. The group's acronym stands for "Niggaz With Attitude": a confrontational moniker designed to provoke. The name promised hard-hitting music, and N.W.A. delivered—the al- bum's content was deemed so offensive that, at first, almost nothing from the group appeared on any radio or television station. Yet the forbidden music so enticed young Americans that *Straight Outta Compton* sold three million records, reaching triple-platinum status through word of mouth alone. In 1991, N.W.A. became the first group to reach number 1 on the *Billboard* pop charts with a style of music known as hard-core "gangsta" rap, a style that now dominates hip-hop at a time when hip-hop is the most vital form of expression for youth culture in the country.

Dre was main architect of the "gangsta" sound. When Dre joined N.W.A. at 21, he had already established himself as one of the premier party DJs in Los Angeles. Just a few years later, after the success of N.W.A., Dre launched a solo career on his own label, Death Row Records, where in the early 1990s, Dre produced a string of albums that sold millions of copies and generated hundreds of millions of dollars in sales.

Gangsta rap's enormous popularity among young Americans of all races and backgrounds provoked an equally grand backlash. N.W.A.'s debut was met with widespread condemnation for their lyrics celebrating murder and mayhem. The question of whether gangsta rap and other such cultural products are good or bad is a debate that no single book can answer. Perhaps the best way to measure Dre's influence is to note the fact that his music became a topic of debate, addressed by members of Congress and presidents during the 1990s. Voices at the highest levels of society declared that gangsta rap should be censored or even banned.

Yet today, for better or worse, gangsta rap has become a part of mainstream American culture. The gangsta aesthetic now dominates hip-hop, making it nearly impossible for rappers to make records unless they can pull off a gangsta image. Dre's protégé, Snoop Doggy Dogg (whose album *Doggystyle* drew calls for censorship when Dre produced it in 1993) now appears in car commercials, using his trademark gangsta rap slang to pitch sedans.

What was it about Dre's music? What is it about his songs that people find so appealing, so shocking, and so irresistible at the same time? Listening to Dre's albums feels like watching a horror movie—we cover our faces, but we peek through our fingers to see what happens next.

All Dre could say was that he knew what he liked: "The music is just in me, you know. That's the only thing I can say. People ask me how I come up with these hits, and I can only say that I know what I like, and I'm quick to tell a motherfucker what I don't like" (Gold, 1993, p. 41).

In the wake of the Los Angeles riots in 1992, Dre made his best music. The two major albums he produced at this time—his own solo debut, *The Chronic* (1992), and Snoop Doggy Dogg's *Doggystyle* (1993)—came to serve as the soundtrack to a grand party in gangsta's paradise, and he solidified for America the image of a life cruising in a drop-top through sunny Southern California. Life, as Dre said in one of his songs, was "nuthin' but a 'G' thang." That captured the imaginations of millions of people, and even those listeners who rightly object to some of Dre's lyrics can hardly help singing along to his memorable hooks.

The influence of Dre's music is an important question, considering the ubiquity of gangsta music and aesthetic we experience every day in our culture. The following chapters set his music and life in a context, to help explain how Dre created the music we now call gangsta and why that makes him one of the most significant figures currently at work in American culture.

Much of Dre's influence comes through his work with the record label he helped create, Death Row Records, the saga of which is one of the most fascinating tales in music history. Beginning with *The Chronic*, Dre produced a string of groundbreaking records for Death Row. Hip-hop critics now call *The Chronic* one of the greatest rap records ever made, and they credit Death Row as the most influential independent record label of the 1990s. This book also covers the dark side of Death Row Records. It's a story about what happens when the life imitates art, when the lines between fantasy and reality blur together; it is a story that ended with the tragic shooting deaths of rappers Tupac Shakur and Biggie Smalls in 1996.

Dre has been more than just a gifted producer, songwriter, rapper, and video director. He also has acted as a talent scout. One of Dre's great joys is discovering underground rappers with unpolished skills and unlimited potential and then turning them into superstar artists. A long list of artists can thank Dre for their careers, and Dre's most celebrated protégés— Snoop Doggy Dogg and Eminem—have become two of the most popular music artists of the twenty-first century.

The hope is that by telling these stories of Dre's life and work, this book will shed some light on the musical roots of West Coast hip-hop, the inner workings of the record industry, and the gangsta phenomenon in America, a subject that has been often discussed but little understood. The goal is that we can then think critically about the culture we inhabit and that our thoughts will become based in facts and history rather than gut reaction alone. We may not share Dre's gift for hearing what's cool, but seeing his music through the eyes of the man who created it may help us better understand the society in which we live.

By the time Andre Young was 24, his hit-making prowess had people talking about Dr. Dre as standing alongside iconic pop producers such as Phil Spector and Quincy Jones. Asked to explain how he does it, Dre only shrugs his shoulders and alludes to his mother's funk and soul record collection that formed his earliest musical influences. Dre's talent for crafting catchy songs with the power to both delight and offend is uniquely his own, a personal flourish on a musical tradition instilled by his family and friends. Scholars note the importance of geography throughout the gangsta rap genre, particularly the California city of Compton in Los Angeles County, Dre's hometown, to which he has brought so much fame.

BORN TO ROCK THE PARTY

Andre Young was born on February 18, 1965, in Compton, a lower-middle-class city that has appeared, in Dre's music, as the primal, sun-soaked setting where his gangsta episodes take place. Dre's parents were divorced before he was born (when he got older, his mother married Warren Griffin Jr., the father of another West Coast rapper, "Warren G," who eventually introduced Dre to the rapper who would become his greatest protégé, Snoop Doggy Dogg). Long before the whole world knew the name Compton, Dre learned the power of music in his family's living room.

Dre's most profound musical influence was his mother. She and her husband were avid fans of the soul and early funk that was popular among African Americans in the mid-1970s. In Dre's house, he has said, the music came on before the lights. The soulful sounds of artists such as James Brown, the Marvelettes, the Temptations, and the Supremes filled the house when Dre was a child, and no doubt, he soon observed how deeply the music affected his parents and their friends. That music captured his imagination.

"I can remember when I was just like about 4 years old in Compton, and my mother would have me stack 45s, stack about 10 of them, and when one would finish, the next record would drop. Do you remember those old record players that played 45s? It was like I was DJing for the house, picking out certain songs and stacking them so this song would go after that song. I would go to sleep with headphones on, listening to music. My mom and my pop—they would have music so loud, loud enough to shake the walls" (Gold, 1993, p. 41).

The young Dre grasped the power of music so quickly that as a boy of 10 or 11, he was allowed the privilege of selecting records at his mother's parties. He enjoyed sitting at the record player until late at night, sifting through his mother's vast collection, picking out songs to match the mood of the party. As a young teenager, Young found himself consumed with music. He committed himself to learning everything he could about it. He listened to records like a student reading a textbook. He took note of how songs were made, honing his ear to the sonic landscape of popular songs, to the way various instruments and sounds interact, and to the architecture of verses, choruses, and bridges, perfecting the sensibility that would inform his own future craft.

Dre was especially drawn to the music that was popular among his friends in the late 1970s: the sounds of funk, particularly George Clinton and his two bands, Parliament and Funkadelic. Mid-1970s funk is such an important foundation of Dre's groundbreaking music (his

signature "G-funk" sound that dominated the 1990s represents his version of Clinton's "P-Funk" sound that dominated the 1970s) that the
genre deserves an overview. Funk truly got the party started, and it is
the foundation for much of hip-hop music today.

THE RHYTHM REVOLUTION

Funk music emerged from the wide-open spirit of the late 1960s. It
was a time when artists of all types felt free to experiment for an audience that craved anything new and exotic. This was especially true of
popular music, where this adventurous attitude combined with new tech-
nologies in musical production and performance—wild guitar sounds,
synthesizers, powerful amplifiers, drum machines, and studio equipment
that could "sample" bits of sound and loop it over and over. Also at this
time, the rock industry developed as the force we know today, so that in
1974, music generated revenues totaling more than $2 billion—nearly
as lucrative as movies ($1.6 billion) and professional sports ($600,000)
combined (Hendler, 1983, p. 165).

Much of Dre's hip-hop is built on a funk beat pioneered largely by the
immortal James Brown. Known as the "Godfather of Soul," Brown introduced funk to mainstream America with the 1965 song "Papa's Got a
Brand New Bag." The innovation of funk could be heard most clearly by
listening to the drummer's high-hat rhythm. Whereas R&B drummers in
the 1940s and 1950s doubled-timed their beats—*da dat, da dat, da dat, da
dat*—to create the skipping rhythm heard in swing jazz or soul, Brown's
drummer laid down an even, driving rhythm—*dat, dat, dat, dat*. The
other instruments accentuated this propulsive rhythm with exclamatory
horn bursts and emotionally charged vamps, creating a music that perfectly complemented Brown's furious dancing style. One of the hallmarks
of gangsta rap is the way Dre uses this funk beat to create feelings of intense momentum and head-bobbing grooves in his music.

Another pioneer of funk in the late 1960s was the group Sly and the
Family Stone. The band's 1969 album *Stand!* was the prototype for mid-
1970s funk bands whose sounds blended danceable funk with the wild
sounds and technical virtuosity of psychedelic and progressive rock. Sly
Stone also set the tone for the "come one, come all" party vibe heard later
in disco, as well as laying the foundation for the social commentary on
urban decay and the Afro-centric themes of black pride expressed in funk.
Much more can be said about Sly Stone, but in our look at the musical
influences of Dre, it is important to know that Sly opened the door for
Dre's most significant influence, George Clinton.

An eccentric and colorful figure, Clinton led two important bands—Parliament and Funkadelic. After moving to New Jersey from his home in North Carolina, Clinton formed Parliament as a slick doo-wop group. When this band floundered, Clinton redesigned the group with outlandish costumes and huge amplifiers. Recording as Funkadelic, the band introduced a sound that combined the beats of James Brown with a guitar wizardry akin to Jimi Hendrix in their groundbreaking debut *Free Your Mind* in 1970 and its follow-up, *Maggot Brain*, in 1971. Three years later, Clinton resurrected Parliament as Funkadelic's more conventional—but no less danceable—alter ego. Clinton and Parliament-Funkadelic ruled the funk scene with albums like *Up for the Down Stroke* (1974), *Mothership Connection* (1975), and *One Nation Under a Groove* (1978). These albums constitute the backbone of much of today's hip-hop, and especially that of Dre. *The Chronic* and Dre's production on Snoop Doggy Dogg's *Doggystyle* are obvious tributes to Clinton's mid-1970s music. The importance of Clinton's music on Dre's work, from the squiggly squealing keyboard lines to the funky bass lines to the crowd-rousing choruses, can hardly be overstated.

GOOD TIMES IN COMPTON

Although funk expressed people's desire to dance and celebrate, many of the lyrics confronted the gritty realities of urban life. The effects of poverty and racism were especially evident in the Compton neighborhood of Los Angeles where Dre grew up. The fact that gangsta rap exploded from the streets of Compton is by no means accidental, so it is important to understand the specific local culture that profoundly influenced Dre's music.

Los Angeles has been an important destination for black migrants since the late 1800s. Many blacks moved into Southern California during an employment boom created there by the expansion of military industry during World War II. During this time, blacks flocked to Los Angeles from states such as Louisiana, Texas, Arkansas, Oklahoma, and Kansas, seeking a chance to earn money, to own property, and to escape the racism prevalent in America, especially in the South.

For these new arrivals, which included popular musicians such as Jelly Roll Morton and Kid Ory, the cultural focus was Central Avenue between 5th Street downtown to 103rd Street Watts. Known as "the Avenue," this boulevard boasted elegant neighborhoods, jazz clubs, and black-owned businesses in a scene some compared to a West Coast version of Harlem, the epicenter of black culture in mid-century. This vibrant black public realm was home to such jazz talents as Charles Mingus, Dexter Gordon, Ornette Coleman, Art Pepper, and Roy Ayers, making Central Avenue a popular destination for hip Los Angeles residents of all races until the mid- to late 1950s.

By the time Andre Young was born in 1965, the scene on Central Avenue was all but extinct. The decline of black cultural life in Los Angeles and in many other American cities involved a complex array of social and personal forces; in Southern California it was a combination of government legislation (specifically, a now-illegal practice called "red-lining," whereby banks denied home loans to blacks based on race; black neighborhoods were outlined in red, and the residents were deemed unfit for lending, which resulted in a large increase in racial segregation in Los Angeles and many other American cities), a declining black economy, and law enforcement policies that contributed to changes in Compton and made it a breeding ground for street gangs.

In Los Angeles, city officials frowned upon various races getting together on the Avenue, enjoying black music at late-night party spots. Officials who wanted blacks and whites to live separately used eminent domain (a law that allows the government to seize private property without the owner's consent, usually for public infrastructure such as roads, but in some cases for a third party, such as a private developer), job discrimination, and red-lining to contain African Americans in specific neighborhoods. During the heyday of Central Avenue, the Los Angeles music scene was controlled by two musicians' unions—one white (union 47) and one black (union 767)—an arrangement that ensured fair treatment for many black musicians. When the two unions integrated in 1953, some black musicians supported the move, but others bitterly opposed it, claiming it gave black musicians fewer chances to work. After the integration of unions 47 and 767, many left Los Angeles for New York City. By 1963, red-lining and job discrimination had hemmed the black population of Los Angeles—some 650,000 people—into the South Central part of the county. The jobs that lured hopeful migrants had disappeared, and by the early 1960s, about 25 percent of black Los Angeles residents lived below the federal poverty line. Economic conditions were exacerbated by poor public transportation that made it even more difficult for people to find work. South Central Los Angeles was a powder keg for discontent, and the fuse was lit by repeated instances of police brutality.

THE LOS ANGELES POLICE DEPARTMENT

In the context of Dre and gangsta rap, one of the most important influences on black life in South Central Los Angeles was the Los Angeles

Police Department. In 1950 the LAPD began incorporating military ideas and tactics with the appointment of Chief William H. Parker. Fueled by the interaction of police with black citizens, Los Angeles artists created a fierce brand of protest poetry that would later influence the confrontational attitude of gangsta rap.

In his book about Los Angeles hip-hop, *It's Not about a Salary*, Brian Cross chronicles a shocking list of instances in which minorities, mostly blacks and Hispanics, were killed by police officers under suspicious circumstances. For example, 60 black citizens were killed by patrolmen between 1963 and 1965–of the 60 victims, 25 were unarmed, and 27 had been shot in the back when they were killed. On August 11, 1965, police arrested a young black man in the Watts neighborhood on a drunk driving charge. A crowd gathered, and a fight with police broke out, quickly escalating into a full-scale riot. By August 17, the so-called Watts Rebellion was quelled, after the unrest had spanned 46 miles, leaving 34 dead, 1,023 wounded, and nearly 4,000 arrested. This led to increasingly harsh tactics from the LAPD, but this time period also saw a new cultural renaissance blossom from the rubble of Central Avenue. The so-called Watts Riots, and the artistic flourish that followed, would be mirrored in Dre's day with the 1992 riots in Los Angeles that prefigured a surge in gangsta rap.

PROTEST POETRY IN LOS ANGELES

In keeping with the spirit of youth energy and political change that swept America in the mid-1960s, South Central Los Angeles was home to a rollicking café culture that included the Black Panthers, the Underground Musicians' Association, the United Slaves, and the Watts Writers' Workshop. Founded in 1965 by Hollywood philanthropist Bud Schulberg, the workshop was a showcase for such African American poets as Odie Hawkins, Quincey Troupe, and the Watts Prophets. Poets from the Watts Workshop were interested in a form of poetry that combined verbal equivalents to improvisational jazz with street slang and a practice known as "toasting" or "playing the dozens," which is now an integral feature of hip-hop.

Toasts are a form of performance poetry that can take the form of jokes, boasts, taunts, or narrative tales. Most often, the subject matter is the life of a "hustler," that is, one who earns his living through illegal or semi-legal activities such as drug dealing, gambling, or managing a group of prostitutes. Originating on street corners and prison yards, toasts featured stories of con games, "turning out" whores, selling drugs, making money, beating adversaries, and flaunting wealth, all delivered in the "street" vernacular of African Americans. In this tradition, artists such as the Last Poets, Gil Scott-Heron, Stanley Crouch, and Nikki Giovanni emerged in the late 1960s. This was a time of "black nationalism," a social and political movement that sought to help African Americans overcome their subjugation in America by emphasizing their identity as people of African ancestry.

Black nationalism and its themes of black pride and black unity made the Watts artists both popular and revolutionary. Their popularity and revolutionary politics drew the attention of the Federal Bureau of Investigation, which infiltrated the organization with an informant in the 1970s. It was a part of the FBI's "Cointelpro" program, a move by FBI director J. Edgar Hoover to identify, disrupt, and destroy progressive community organizations such as the Watts Writers' Workshop. Some scholars blame the FBI's tactics for the disintegration of the Watts Writers' Workshop in the mid-1970s.

Also emerging from this new artistic milieu in Los Angeles was filmmaker Melvin Van Peebles. His 1970 film *Sweet Sweetback's Badaaasss Song* was a milestone in the development of hip-hop. The movie tells the story of a black sex worker who kills two police officers to save a black activist and then goes on the run from Watts to Mexico to escape the wrath of the law. The gritty realism and thumping funk soundtrack spawned inferior but popular films in a genre known as "blaxploitation"—films such as *Dolemite* and *Superfly,* which heavily influenced Dre's interest in confrontational lyrics and themes.

Although Dre's music retained the sense of outrage and the explicit language of the black artists who emerged from South Central Los Angeles, he roundly rejected one important aspect of its content—political activism, which at that time seemed stale to Dre and other people his age. One of the elements of Dre's music that made it seem so "authentic" to his listeners was that the music contained no specific political message. In fact, Dre specifically intended his songs to be an alternative to the overt political themes common in the late 1960s and 1970s, messages that by the 1980s had begun to seem to many in Dre's generation like so much empty preaching. "I wanted to make people go: 'Oh shit, I can't believe he's sayin' that shit'; I wanted to go all the way left, everybody trying to do this black power and shit, so I was like let's give 'em an alternative, nigger, niggernigger niggernigger, fuck this fuck that, bitch bitch bitch bitch, suck my dick, all this kind of shit, you know what I'm saying" (Cross, 1993, p. 197).

NEW YORK CITY AND THE BIRTH OF HIP-HOP

As a young teenager, when Andre Young graduated from spinning records in his mother's living room to attending parties while a student at

Centennial High School in Compton, the songs most likely to be pumping on the dance floor were funk hits from bands like Parliament and Funkadelic. At that time, in the late 1970s, a new style of music was just beginning to emerge from New York City, a genre that would become known as hip-hop and constitute perhaps the most important development in American music culture in the past 30 years.

BREAK BEATS, BACKSPINS, FLY RHYMES, AND SPRAY PAINT

Hip-hop culture is defined by four elements: DJing, rapping, break dancing, and graffiti art. Originally seen by the music industry as a fad, today hip-hop is one of the most significant features of American culture.

The hip-hop revolution began in the Bronx in New York City, with a DJ named Clive Campbell (aka Kool Herc). After performing his first DJ gig at his sister's birthday party in 1973, in the recreation room of the family's West Bronx housing project, Herc performed at parks and block parties with an enormous sound system, which he modeled after the mobile speaker units he'd seen in his native Jamaica. At the time, DJs kept people dancing by using two turntables—a skillful DJ cut from one turntable to the other, seamlessly blending one song into the next. Whereas most New York DJs spun trendy disco hits, Herc catered to the tastes of his mostly black and Hispanic audiences by playing the funk anthems from the mid-1970s, the favorites that disco had pushed aside. While playing hits from the likes of James Brown, Sly Stone, and George Clinton, Herc noticed that people went especially wild during the "break" segments, when the drums and percussion sections took over the song. In an experimental mood, Herc took two copies of the same record and cut back and forth between them in order to prolong the break, or the sonic climax. In the process, he created the innovation known as the "break beat," using the turntable to create an intense, repetitive drum pattern. The break beat strips down music to a form that is almost strictly rhythm, creating a deep, dance-inducing groove. As a musical innovation, the break beat resembled punk (which was also developing at the time), deconstructed the lavish production aesthetic of the 1970s, and reduced music to a fundamental form, creating sounds and songs that felt raw and powerful—indeed, hip-hop and rock continue to share influences and audience.

Hip-hop's characteristic break dancing developed when Herc's break beat inspired a following of dancers who saved their best moves for these rhythmic climaxes. Herc's dancing devotees became known as "break boys," or "b-boys." Rap, another element of hip-hop culture, developed as people grabbed microphones to exhort the crowd to get up, dance, put their hands in the air, and have fun. Known as MCs ("masters of ceremony" or "mike controllers"), early rappers in New York included Coke La Rock, Luvbug Starski, and Busy Bee. Underprivileged kids in the Bronx couldn't get past the bouncers at upscale Manhattan dance clubs, but they could slip out of the house to go see Herc perform with the MCs and the b-boys at the neighborhood park.

One of these kids was a high school student named Afrika Bambaataa, leader of the Black Spades, the largest, most notorious street gang ruling the rough streets of the South Bronx. Even as the leader of a sometimes violent street gang, Bambaataa organized what he called the Zulu Nation, a group made up of several housing projects whose residents united to reduce the threat of drugs and crime. The Zulu Nation was founded on lofty principles—knowledge, wisdom, freedom, justice, and peace—but Bambaataa knew how to throw a good party, too. At these parties in parks and housing-project community rooms, the Zulu Nation promulgated the four art forms that came to be known collectively as hip-hop: rapping, DJing, break dancing, and graffiti.

By 1975, Bronx street gangs were disbanding under the weight of drugs, violence, and police crackdown. In its place, hip-hop culture was spreading among the working-class and lower-middle-class neighborhoods of New York. Much of hip-hop music as we know it today was pioneered by Grandmaster Flash and the Furious Five. Flash, a DJ, perfected the technique of "scratching," using the otherwise annoying sound of a needle moving back and forth on a record to create a rhythmic sound. Flash was also the first to use a machine called a "beat box," a manually operated drum machine; and he was the first to use MCs not just as accompaniment to the DJ, but as performers in and of themselves. By 1978, MCs such as the Bronx's Cold Crush Brothers and the Mighty Force Emcees had replaced DJs as the stars of hip-hop. In 1979, Sugar Hill Records released rap's first hit single, "Rapper's Delight," by a group called the Sugar Hill Gang. Using rhymes taken from other New York rappers (who received no credit and no share of the song's profits) and the rhythm track from Chic's disco hit "Good Times," "Rapper's Delight" eventually became a top-10 hit and introduced America to the phrase "hip-hop."

HIP-HOP HITS LOS ANGELES

In 1980, when Andre Young was 15 years old, he and other young music fans in Los Angeles heard "Rapper's Delight" on the radio, and they saw Afrika Bambaataa, who brought his group Soul Sonic Force there on tour that year. When the Rock Steady Crew visited Los Angeles in 1982, they brought a group of East Coast DJs, MCs, and break-dancers. The New Yorkers discovered that the West Coast had already developed its own perspective on the hip-hop arts. The most obvious L.A. innovation was a funky type of dancing influenced by modern technology—a style the Californians called popping and locking.

Hip-hop scholar Brian Cross describes the dance's origins in Los Angeles in the early 1970s. The "locking" style is named for the way the dancers lock their joints, and its popularity grew along with gang culture in South Central Los Angeles. "Popping" is based on the moves of a robot, typified by extraordinary body control and influenced by animation, machines, and traditional mime techniques. The popularity of popping and locking subsided in the 1970s, but when New York break-dancers brought their dancing to town, people in Los Angeles revived their tradition. In the early 1980s, Hollywood produced the movies *Flashdance* and *Breakin'*, which, along with independent films such as *Wild Style* and *Breaking and Entering*, turned breaking, popping, and locking into a single fad that came to be known across America as break dancing.

In Los Angeles, the emerging hip-hop culture found roots in an all-ages club called Radio that opened downtown in 1982. The club introduced a large and diverse crowd of Californians to the latest hip-hop hits from the New York underground. Los Angeles music fans fondly remember Radio and another early hip-hop club, Radiotron, as part of a time before Los Angeles hip-hop came to be associated with violence and potential gunplay.

Just as important as clubs in the development of West Coast hip-hop was the car. Hip-hop is closely related to the specific places where the artists live—whereas New Yorkers experienced hip-hop in large park jams, in Los Angeles such public concerts could only be carried out under the watchful eye of city authorities and police. Los Angeles has a long tradition of car culture: the Beach Boys, for example, had a string of hits about cruising in cars along palm-lined beach boulevards. Car culture is enormously popular in Los Angeles and—because of a woeful public transportation system—unavoidable. Graffiti in Los Angeles appears on highway overpasses instead of on subway trains. By the time Dre started making music in the early 1980s, his friends had their own up-to-date versions of the hot rods celebrated in Beach Boys hits. Dre designed his music to sound best when it came blasting from the sound system of his friends' "kitted-out rides."

Indeed, car culture was a huge influence on the music of Dr. Dre. "I make shit for people to bump in their cars," he said. "When I do a mix, the first thing I do is go down and see how it sounds in the car" (Cross, 1993, p. 197).

Los Angeles also had its own versions of Kool Herc and his traveling sound system shows. In the early 1980s, a traveling group of DJs calling themselves Uncle Jam's Army (named for a Funkadelic album) took music into the neighborhoods. Using a much more technologically advanced system than Herc's, Uncle Jam's Army could put on much larger shows in sports arenas and convention centers.

MICROPHONE CHECK

Rapping is a combination of speech, poetry, and song, with rhymes delivered rhythmically either to a beat or a cappella. Today, rapping is one of the central elements of hip-hop culture and music, although the practice of rapping is centuries old. Folk poets of West Africa used rhyme and rhythm, accompanied by sparse instrumentation or drumming, to tell epic stories. Modern rap has also been influenced by the improvisational spirit of jazz music, and many rappers and scholars cite the "scat" singing of jazz as an important influence on rap.

The hip-hop raps we hear today developed in school playgrounds, on buses, and in lunchrooms, with young MCs challenging each other in a battle to see who was the better rhymer. Usually, battlers would use instrumental tracks from record labels such as Sugarhill/Enjoy or Uni, imitating the meters of the original rhymers, but changing the words to describe local situations or to alter the meaning of the original in humorous ways. Another important skill for any true rapper is the art of "freestyle," where rappers are able to create and perform original rhymes on the spot, off the top of their heads. Roller rinks, such as World on Wheels and Skateland in Compton, were other popular sites for hip-hop DJs and MCs, including a young Dre.

As a teenage music fan, Andre Young was following the new hip-hop trend closely. He was learning how to DJ, and he adopted the name "Dr. Dre" in homage to his favorite basketball player, Julius "Dr. J" Erving of the Philadelphia 76ers. Dre played high school parties, spinning funk and early hip-hop. He started hanging around outside a club called Eve After Dark, a new Compton club that did not serve alcohol, but enforced an age limit, and this was where Dre found his first real job as a DJ—and made the connections that would propel him from Compton to the national stage.

Chapter 2

DRE GOES WORLD CLASS

Dre was always looking for a chance to take his next step forward. Spinning records at high school parties was fun, but Dre wanted to make important hip-hop records. To get that chance, he needed a more professional atmosphere where he could develop his talent; he needed a regular gig.

ALONZO WILLIAMS'S NEWEST STAR

An ambitious teenager, Dre set his sights on the hottest club in Compton: Eve After Dark. There, a regular DJ gig belonged to a hard-driving dancer and singer named Alonzo Williams, who got behind the turntables to make money. He worked block parties and, as the crowds grew larger, graduated to 1,000-seat venues such as Alpine Village in Torrance and even the Queen Mary. In the early 1980s, Williams landed a regular gig spinning records at Eve from 9 p.m. on Friday until 5 in the morning, playing to three or four different crowds. To share the work, Williams assembled a team of DJs called Disco Construction. As the disco fad died, Williams changed his group's name to the World Class Wreckin' Cru, named for the piles of equipment they had to tear down after each show. Eve was a classy club—women wore dresses; men wore ties and slacks. Williams and his DJs wore Jeri-curl hairstyles, dressed in matching lavender outfits, and danced in Temptation-style choreography. They played hits of the time—Donna Summer, Average White Band, George Clinton, Parliament, and Prince. "People came out in droves," Williams said. "It was a constant party" (McDermott, 2002, p. 14).

Because of Eve's age limit, the 17-year-old Dre had to hang around outside, pleading with Williams to give him a tryout with the group. Williams always refused—until one night, when one of his DJs had to miss the show.

In L.A.'s competitive DJ scene, the key to success, Williams said, was to "find the most obscure record you could and play it" (McDermott, 2002, p. 14). Dre was young, but Williams was impressed by his vast musical knowledge. The first time he let Dre work the turntables, Dre delivered a mix of the soul classic "Wait a Minute, Mr. Postman" driven by the beat of Afrika Bambaataa's hip-hop anthem "Planet Rock." The two songs are completely different in terms of mood and rhythm, but Dre made them work together, and the crowd loved it. "I would put together this mix shelf, lots of oldies, Martha and the Vandellas and stuff like that," says Dre. "And where normally you go to a club and the DJs play all the hit records back to back, I used to put on a serious show. People would come from everywhere, just to see Dr. Dre on the wheels of steel" (Gold, 1993, p. 42). Williams took note. Not only did Dre possess musical talent, but he was also young and good-looking, more assets that Williams thought would make the Wreckin' Cru a bigger draw on the party scene.

Dre took to Williams as something of an "older brother" figure. Williams helped Dre with money management—a skill at which Dre was remarkably poor—and the Wreckin' Cru studio was like a home away from home for Dre (his stepfather once gave Dre and his friends karate lessons in the studio).

Along with his own band, Williams also booked other acts at Eve, including the first California appearances of such New York hip-hop stars as Kurtis Blow and Run-DMC. When the Wreckin' Cru saw the groundbreaking Run-DMC for the first time, the group members stood around staring at each other in amazement.

The members of the Wreckin' Cru began writing their own material. Never mind that no one in the group actually knew how to play an instrument—Cru member Antoine "DJ Yella" Carraby knew how to program a drum machine, and Dre had a natural musicianship and a sense of how to create a song that most DJs could only dream of.

During the day, Dre and Yella hung out at Eve. They listened to records, learning how to reproduce instrumental tracks on an old four-track recording deck in the back room. In 1984 the Cru went into Audio Achievements studio in Torrance and spent $100 to record two tracks: "Slice" and "Kru Groove." The music featured fast, driving techno rhythms influenced by the German electronic group Kraftwerk and their 1976 hit "Autobahn." The tracks were mostly programmed on the drum machine by Dre and Yella, including the distinctive "wicka-wicka" sound of turntable scratching. Another member of the Cru, a rapper named Marquette Hawkins and known as Cli-N-Tel, provided lyrics (mostly celebrating the skills of Dre and Yella).

Williams took the recordings to a company called Macola Records, an independent Hollywood label that pressed as few as 500 records at a time. This allowed up-and-coming artists like the Cru to make their own products for a relatively small investment. The Cru began selling their two-sided, 12-inch dance single out of the trunk of Williams's car all across Los Angeles. They eventually sold about 5,000 copies, an impressive number for an operation of this sort.

PROBLEMS WITH MONEY

An important site for Dre and early L.A. hip-hop was the Roadium on Redondo Beach Boulevard in Torrance. The Roadium was an abandoned drive-in that by 1985 had become the site of one of the largest "swap meets" in Los Angeles. A swap meet is simply a huge public market, featuring secondhand items, including clothes, furniture, and car parts; food; and vendors peddling wares of all kinds.

Swap meets were the perfect places for up-and-coming artists like Williams—people with no record contract, no money for marketing and advertising, and no deal to have their work distributed in stores—to sell their product. On the swap-meet circuit, Williams met Steve Yano, a former psychology graduate student who ran a popular stall selling underground records at the Roadium on weekends. The meeting was a turning point for Dre's career.

Yano spent his weeks scouring the used record bins across Los Angeles to find items to sell. Because most of his customers at the Roadium were African American, Yano started looking for the records that his customers were asking about—Kurtis Blow, Run-DMC, Grandmaster Flash. When the DJ craze hit Los Angeles, Williams became one of Yano's best sources for brand-new tracks. One day, Yano met Williams at Eve After Dark, and there he heard Dre and Yella in one of their practice sessions.

Yano listened intently, captivated by the way Dre and Yella made music with a drum machine and a turntable. The two made a tape for Yano, who played it at the swap meet that weekend, and people started asking where they could get their own copies.

The Cru followed up their successful 12-inch record with "Surgery," a song produced by Dre that sold 50,000 copies—an eye-popping total for a record that was independently produced and distributed. The music was classic Cru—bare-bones electronic funk, fast drum-machine beats, turntable scratching, and goofy lyrics. After "Surgery," the Wreckin' Cru produced another single, "Juice," followed by a 1985 album called *World Class*.

The album caught the attention of a CBS record executive named Larkin Arnold, who requested a meeting with Williams. The meeting went well, and CBS sent the Wreckin' Cru on tour as an opening act for funk icon Rick James. While on the road, Williams got a call from his lawyer, with the news that CBS was offering a record contract with a $100,000 advance. They were one of the first early hip-hop acts in Los Angeles to get a big contract, but today, Williams looks back on the deal ruefully.

"It was the worst thing that ever happened," he says. "From that point on, we had nothing but dissension over money" (McDermott, 2002, p. 15). The loudest complaints came from Dre. He was the musical backbone of Wreckin' Cru, but he wasn't getting paid nearly as much as Williams. In his defense, Williams says that Dre and other members of the group didn't understand how much he had to pay to keep the group going—money for advertising, recording, travel, and equipment. Yet, ironically, as the group grew more successful, their arguments over money became more intense.

Dre's relationship with Williams followed a pattern that would then be repeated several times in Dre's musical career. Dre is a supremely talented artist, with a gift for entering a recording studio and emerging with hit music. In the studio, Dre was always the boss. But Dre was a poor manager of his own money, and he seemed to need big-brother figures like Williams to handle his business affairs. In his relationships with N.W.A. and Death Row records, Dre trusted first Eazy-E, and then Suge Knight, to handle business while he made the hit songs. Like the Wreckin' Cru, Dre would leave N.W.A. and Death Row over conflicts with these big-brother figures.

KDAY

Critical to Dre's development as an artist was the emergence of KDAY in Los Angeles, the first radio station to adopt a hip-hop format. Program director Greg Mack came to Los Angeles in 1983 when KDAY's owners hired him to change the station's format. Mack started playing rap in the evenings, and he introduced Los Angeles listeners to artists such as Run-DMC, the Fat Boys, and one of the first gangsta rappers, a former Los Angeles street hustler–turned–MC who went by the name Ice-T. He developed a program called "Mixmasters" to spotlight local rappers. Dre and his Wreckin' Cru bandmate, Yella, worked as KDAY's first in-house DJs for the popular show, and, as Mack says, "their careers just skyrocketed" (Cross, 1993, p. 155).

Dre started playing mixes 15 minutes every day on KDAY's five o'clock show, "Traffic Jam." He churned out mixes at a fast and furious pace, which helped Dre hone his craft. "I did like fifty mixes for him . . . . It definitely helped me out producing. Those mixes were wild, each like a little record. KDAY was the shit, they put a lot of people on the map, they definitely put N.W.A. on the map" (Cross, 1993, p. 198).

As the Los Angeles scene was waiting to explode, there was evidence almost immediately that L.A.'s gang culture would be a prominent aspect of West Coast hip-hop. When KDAY and Mack hosted a Run-DMC concert in Long Beach, fights broke out between rival gangs. The fights turned into a full-scale confrontation that drew police cars and helicopters, and the incident made national news. "It was the worst I've ever seen in my life," says Mack. Fear of gang violence in L.A. prompted many clubs to refuse hip-hop acts, and it looked as if the issue would hamper West Coast hip-hop. "Everywhere they tried, things would just get messed up," says Mack. "There was always something" (Cross, 1993, p. 157).

INFLUENCES

As an artist, Dre was able to transform the violent aspects of Los Angeles street culture into a style of music that brought worldwide fame to Dre and Compton. His group, N.W.A., used images of gang life in a way that reshaped the hip-hop landscape, stealing the spotlight from the East Coast and turning it west.

It would be a mistake, however, to assume that when Dre invented the hip-hop genre known as gangsta rap that he was drawing only from this kind of gang violence that he witnessed. In fact, Dre drew from the albums and movies that captured his attention while growing up in California. Through the influence on a generation of creative young people, the following artists and cultural products contributed significantly to gangsta rap and much of today's hip-hop sound.

Richard Pryor

When N.W.A.'s album *Elif4zaggin* hit number 1 on the *Billboard* chart in 1991, it marked the first time an album with the word "nigger" in the title had gone top 10 since Richard Pryor's *Bicentennial Nigger* in 1976. The language in Pryor's legendary live comedy performances seemed just as shocking as Cube's raps, and indeed Cube cites Pryor as an important

influence when he began rapping with Dre. Listeners who get beyond Pry-
or's rough language find scathing, irreverent, hilarious comedy and sharp
insights into society. He riffed on race relations, sex, politics, religion, and
drug abuse with such candor that his own record label filed an injunc-
tion to stop the release of Pryor's third, breakthrough album, *That Nigger's
Crazy* (1974). After a visit to Africa in 1979, a rich and successful Pryor
swore he would never use the "n-word" on stage again. Before his death in
2005 after a long battle with Parkinson's Disease, Pryor appeared in more
than 40 films, won several Grammy Awards for his albums and Emmy
Awards for his television writing, and in 1998 became the first recipient
of the Mark Twain Award for Humor.

George Clinton

Listen to Dre's 1992 gangsta rap masterpiece, *The Chronic*, and you will
find it impossible to deny the musical influence of George Clinton. The
music Clinton made with his two groups, Funkadelic (a psychedelic blend
of rock and funk) and Parliament (funkier than Funkadelic, with less rock
influence) helped define the 1970s. Many of Clinton's beats and bass lines
have been sampled and borrowed for countless hip-hop songs, and Dre
drew most heavily from two Parliament albums—*Up for the Down Stroke*
(1974) and *Chocolate City* (1976). Clinton's 1982 hit "Atomic Dog" provided the signature sound for Dre's album with Snoop Doggy Dogg, *Doggystyle* (1993). Clinton's influences on gangsta have been good for his
career in recent years—more than any other 1970s funkster, Clinton has
enjoyed enduring popularity among rock listeners. He produced the 1985
Red Hot Chili Peppers album *Freaky Styley* and appeared on the bill for
the Lollapalooza art-rock festival in 1994.

Scarface

This 1983 film written by Oliver Stone and directed by Brian De Palma
has had a profound influence on the content of much hip-hop music, particularly gangsta rap. The movie tells the story of Tony Montana (played
by Al Pacino), a fictional Cuban refugee who rises to the top of Miami's
criminal underworld during the American cocaine boom of the 1980s, before a climactic downfall. The movie generated controversy for its harsh
language and graphic violence, and many hip-hop artists cite Montana's
story as a reflection of their own rise from poverty to wealth. Lines from
the film often appear in hip-hop lyrics, and Brad Jordan, a rapper for the
Houston-based gangsta rap group Geto Boys, named himself Scarface

after the film. References to the movie appear commonly in countless other movies, television shows, and video games.

Dolemite

Stand-up comedian Rudy Ray Moore developed the character Dolemite and co-wrote the 1975 film *Dolemite*. The film belonged to (or, perhaps, parodied) a genre known as "blaxploitation," so called because of such films' exaggerated portrayal of African American stereotypes. Moore developed the character based on a traditional urban "toast," or oral story. The film portrays an ex-con who attempts to settle old scores with fellow inmates with an assembled band of beautiful women skilled in kung-fu. The movie earned cult fame despite (or perhaps because of) its amusingly inept production and odd blend of comedy and action. The language and humor of Dolemite has been a major influence on hip-hop and gangsta rap; Dolemite specifically appears in a memorable verse from Dre's hit "Nuthin' But a 'G' Thang," when Snoop Doggy Dogg boasts that his ability to collect money and girlfriends rivals that of the iconic character.

Chapter 3

STRAIGHT OUTTA COMPTON

As a member of the World Class Wreckin' Cru, Dre established himself as one of the premier hip-hop DJs in Los Angeles while still in his early twenties. Alonzo Williams, leader of the Wreckin' Cru, hoped Dre would bring his band fame and fortune, but Dre had different ideas.

He wanted to make hard-core rap inspired by the rough language and humor of the street life he saw in Compton. When Dre turned 20 years old in 1985, it was a time when the majority of music broadcast on radio and television seemed, to Dre, not "real." Indeed, by the mid-1980s, the rock and pop industry were becoming increasingly sophisticated in their strategies for producing and marketing hit songs. Many of the songs on the *Billboard* Top 40 were produced by corporate songwriters working from expensive market research on exactly the type of sound and image young people wished to buy.

Of course, songs produced through focus groups for mass appeal can seem too safe for teenage listeners, like a toy with no hard edges. In trying to make music that will appeal to as many people as possible, big record companies often ignore the newest sounds coming from the most innovative artists. Mainstream pop usually fails to capture the feelings of young people, who turn to "underground" music to find sounds that will speak to their experiences, fantasies, and tastes, music that will shock their parents.

It's hard to imagine anything more shocking to parents at the time than *Straight Outta Compton*. N.W.A.'s debut record, released in 1989, is now considered to be the first important album Dre produced. The album is considered a classic today, but it was made on a shoestring budget "just so we could have something to sell out of the trunk," Dre said later (Gold, 1993, p. 124). The story of N.W.A. and of the making of *Straight Outta Compton* charts the album's unlikely journey from the trunk of Dre's car to the shelves of record stores across America.

"YOU BETTER GET UP AND ROCK"

Joining the World Class Wreckin' Cru was a good career move for Dre. The gig at Eve After Dark meant steady money and local fame and—more importantly—access to studio music-making equipment and a nightclub laboratory to test the crowd's response to the original music he composed.

Yet Dre had no interest in the Wreckin' Cru's aesthetic style. He thought the music sounded weak and dated—not "real" enough to speak to Dre and his friends in Compton. Perhaps even less tolerable for Dre than Williams's tastes in music was his taste in stage fashion: Williams dressed his band in matching outfits that included lace shirts, white gloves, and eyeliner. Feeling that Williams and the rest of the Wreckin' Cru didn't listen to his ideas, the 17-year-old Dre decided to go with the flow, make some money, and bide his time until a better opportunity came along.

Dre wanted to make music influenced by P-Funk—the hard-core funk style developed by George Clinton and his bands Parliament and Funkadelic—and spiced with the dramatic language and imagery of Los Angeles gang life, and the Wreckin' Cru was not the band where he would get the opportunity to do that. While looking for a different outlet for his talents, Dre found someone to share his vision. O'Shea Jackson was three years younger than Dre, and he had been writing rhymes since the fourth grade. He lived just a few doors away from Dre's cousin, Sir Jinx, and rapped in a group with Jinx called CIA (Criminals in Action), for which Dre produced some songs. Dre and Jackson (who rapped under the stage name Ice Cube) both loved Richard Pryor, Dolomite, and hip-hop, and they made for a good partnership. Dre took Cube under his wing and became an artistic mentor, bringing him along to perform with him at clubs and to the recording studio at Eve After Dark. The pair's favorite act involved remaking popular hits into naughty parodies—the Run-D.M.C. hit "My Adidas," for example, became "My Penis" after Cube retooled the lyrics. Dre was performing as a DJ at parties and roller rinks in Compton. In front of potentially tough crowds at places such as the Skateland roller rink, Dre and Cube mastered the art of winning over an audience. "I would tell him that with this crowd, you better get up and rock," says Dre. "Because if you didn't, they'd throw these full cups at your ass. I would have Cube and my cousin change the words to certain songs, and the crowd would get going, and I'd be mixing. That was the dope" (Gold, 1993, p. 42).

The experience taught the pair an important lesson. "We knew the value of language, especially profanity," says Cube. "We weren't that sophisticated, but we knew the power it had" (McDermott, 2002, p. 16).

THE ROADIUM SWAP MEET

The way Dre and Cube got the crowds going caught the attention of a young would-be entrepreneur named Eric "Eazy-E" Wright. Their partnership was a turning point for Dre and for the history of hip-hop.

Wright was a small-time drug dealer with a little money saved up from selling cocaine, and he was looking for a way to invest his money in something legal. If all else failed, Wright planned to follow in his father's footsteps and become a postman, but before doing so, he wanted to take a shot at getting rich in the music business. He recognized the lucrative potential of hard-core rap and decided to start a record company. The first thing he would need is music, and by this time, Dre had already distinguished himself as one of the hottest producers in Los Angeles. Wright began scheming a way to get Dre to record some songs for him.

Wright started by doing his homework. In 1985 the places to find underground hip-hop music in Los Angeles were swap meets. At the popular Roadium swap meet in Torrence, Wright met music peddler Steve Yano, a thin Japanese man and former high-school guidance counselor who, through his music stall at the Roadium, unwittingly changed the course of popular music.

While a graduate student in educational psychology at Cal State in Los Angeles, Yano had worked in a record store, eventually becoming part owner. When his partner sold the store, Yano took his payment in merchandise and started selling records at swap meets. Most of the clientele at the Roadium were African American, so Yano started tailoring his stock to match his customers' tastes. He had everything—all the new East Coast hip-hop, the best R&B from the late 1960s and early 1970s, Los Angeles dance jams, and music that no other record store had and that few people had ever even heard of.

In an interview with Terry McDermott of the *Los Angeles Times*, Yano recalled the day Eric Wright first visited his stall. Wright was a little guy, no more than 5'6", with a slow swagger. Yano saw him going through big piles of his 12-inch records, including one from the World Class Wreckin' Cru. Wright had a high, squeaky voice that made him sound younger than he looked, and he already looked young. Yano couldn't believe he could have enough money to buy this many records at a time—people who shopped at the Roadium didn't have a lot of money. They wouldn't be there if they did. Wright pulled a roll of cash out of his sock, paid for the records, and asked Yano to relay a message to Dre: "Tell Dre, Eric says, 'Whassup?'" (McDermott, 2002, p. 12).

Yano sold many of the mixes that Dre and fellow Wreckin' Cru member DJ Yella concocted in their studio at Eve After Dark. Yano, however, didn't bother Dre with Wright's request. Yet Wright kept coming back to see Yano, every weekend, politely but persistently asking for Dre's number. Finally, Yano asked Dre if he knew somebody named Eric Wright. He did. Wright wanted to open a record store, but Yano advised him against it. Dre, meanwhile, was pestering Yano to start a record label, a place where Dre could produce and sell his own music. So Yano helped Wright and Dre connect, helping these dreams converge.

Like many important changes in Dre's career, this one occurred largely because of problems with money.

HARD TIMES FOR THE CRU

Even when the Wreckin' Cru was earning money from their tour and a record deal with CBS, Dre seemed forever broke and simply ignored financial matters whenever he could, spending his money on clothes and good times. Dre consistently racked up piles of tickets for parking and traffic violations, and he never paid them until the fines doubled, tripled, and eventually landed him in jail. Williams bailed Dre out time and again. "What you gonna do? Couldn't leave him in jail," says Wreckin' Cru manager Williams. "You might have a gig that weekend" (McDermott, 2002, p. 16).

This arrangement worked well enough until the Wreckin' Cru fell on leaner times. The final split between Dre and the Wreckin' Cru came when Dre called Williams from jail, once again. On this occasion, Dre owed Williams money for a car. According to Williams, he had sold Dre his old Mazda RX-7, which eventually was stolen, and Dre had missed payments to Williams. The Wreckin' Cru wasn't performing so many gigs now, and nobody in the group had a lot of money.

Finally, Williams told Dre he wouldn't help him get out of jail. So Dre called Eazy-E, and Eazy agreed to pay Dre's bail. Dre eventually paid his debt to Williams by producing tracks for the Wreckin' Cru that turned out to be minor hits: a single with the songs "House Calls" and "Cabbage Patch," released in 1987, and a slow jam called "Before You Turn Out the

Lights," which became a hit on the rhythm and blues charts in 1988. But Dre's time with the Wreckin' Cru was coming to an end, leaving Williams feeling as if Eazy was prying Dre away from him. Williams also knew Dre was tired of the Wreckin' Cru and tired of the slow ballads, the flashy costumes, and the choreographed dances. Dre seemed enticed by Eazy's lifestyle, and he wanted to be a rapper.

Eazy explained the situation this way, with his characteristically businesslike outlook: "You see him, where he is now and you see me where I am now? Lonzo had more than me in the beginning, he had a house and a car, and thought he was the shit. That fuckin' lipstick and lace and boxers and shit didn't last too long" (Cross, 1993, p. 202).

EAZY DOES IT

Wright took Yano's advice against opening a record store, and set his entrepreneurial sights on founding a record label. He had a name—Ruthless Records—and with Dre, he secured tracks from one of the West Coast's hottest DJs.

The first song for Ruthless Records was going to be "Boyz in the Hood," a rap Ice Cube wrote during high school English class about the adventures of a young gang member in Compton. Dre hoped to record a New York rap duo called HBO performing "Boyz in the Hood." Eazy booked studio time at Audio Achievements, the same Los Angeles studio where the Wreckin' Cru had recorded their songs. "I had Ice Cube write this song for these guys 'cause I didn't like the way they wrote songs," says Dre (Cross, 1993, p. 197). The members of HBO didn't like the new lyrics, however, and they abandoned the effort. That left Dre in an empty studio with a song and no rapper, so he persuaded Eazy-E to take the microphone and give music a try.

BOYZ N THA HOOD

The song, titled "Boyz N Tha Hood" in its completed version, tells the story of a young man's adventures during a single day: It begins with the narrator cruising down the street in his car. He shoots a friend for trying to steal his car stereo, he fights with his girlfriend and her father, and then he wrecks his car and walks home. It was a compelling story, but Eazy knew absolutely nothing about rapping, and it showed. It took two days to record the one song, and Eazy's thin, high-pitched voice was completely different than the deep, aggressive tone displayed by almost every other rapper. "We all laughed cuz it was so bad," Williams recalls (McDermott, 2002, p. 16).

"Boyz N Tha Hood" was not the first "gangsta" rap song. Philadelphia's Schoolly D and New York's KRS-One had already rapped about the trials and tribulations of pimps and spun lurid tales of gang violence, but there was something different about Eazy's unpracticed delivery. His tone was cold and dispassionate, not theatrical, making him seem more like a real person than a performing entertainer. Moreover, earlier gangsta raps often included cautionary tales about the dangers of the hustler's life; however, Eazy-E (rapping Ice Cube's lyrics) spoke of violence and crime in a way that showed no remorse, no sense of judgment or consequences. According to this perspective, things just happened, as if the individual had no control of his or her own fate.

Eazy didn't know anything about rapping, but he did know how to sell records (sometimes practicing a business ethic he no doubt picked up in cocaine deals). In 1986, Eazy paid Macola $7,000 for 10,000 12-inch singles. This allowed producers Dre and Eazy to make a record for relatively little money—but it wasn't cheap enough for Wright. According to Lorenzo Patterson, a rapper Eazy recruited for Ruthless, Wright would go to the Macola offices under the pretense of meeting with owner Don MacMillan and then would sneak into the back room and steal copies of his own record. Wright also hired friends as "snipers," to take the records around to neighborhood record stores and give away cassettes to kids who were the leaders of local cliques and gangs. At his stall at the Roadium, Yano could hardly keep "Boyz N Tha Hood" in stock. Wright's street-level marketing strategy worked just as well for gangsta rap as it had for narcotics. Improbable as it seemed, "Boyz N Tha Hood" became an underground hit.

The success of "Boyz N Tha Hood" indicated that the young artists might be onto a hit formula. Bolstered by the song's success, Eazy persuaded Dre, Cube, and DJ Yella to form a group. They recruited another local rapper named Kim Nazell, known as the Arabian Prince. He was soon replaced by Patterson, who took the stage name MC Ren, and Tray Curray, who performed as the D.O.C. Eazy's pitch to the group was straightforward. At Ruthless, they could make records that other companies wouldn't touch—records like "Boyz N Tha Hood," full of sex, fights, drinking, and drugging. Yella, at 24, was the oldest person in the group. Eazy was 23 at the time; Dre, 21; Ren, 20; and Cube, just 18.

While hanging out at the Arabian Prince's house in Inglewood, they came up with a name for the new group. Trying to think of a name that would identify them as hailing from the West Coast, someone suggested From Compton with Love, but that wouldn't do. Eazy suggested Niggaz With Attitude, which could be shortened to N.W.A.

In an interview with *Vibe* magazine, Cube recalled hearing about the name that would change his life. "Dre and Eazy picked me up in the van and they was like 'You know what we gonna call the group?' I was like, 'What?' and they said, 'Niggaz With Attitude.'" Cube remembers feeling surprised. "Niggaz With Attitude? Ain't nobody going to put that out," said Cube. "Dre said, 'We'll break it down to N.W.A. and wait till people ask.' Sounded like a plan" (Light, 1999, p. 257).

FROM THE CALIFORNIA RAISINS TO N.W.A.

At this point, Ice Cube surprised the group by leaving Los Angeles to study architectural drafting in Arizona, telling the group he wanted practical job training in case the music gig didn't work out. When he returned, he discovered that Eazy had made some important connections in the music business, and it quickly became apparent that Cube's money would come from his voice, not his hands.

Eazy began pestering Alonzo Williams to introduce him to Jerry Heller, a talent manager who signed many West Coast artists, trying to sift out potential hits. Williams was no friend of Eazy, suspecting that he was trying to steal Dre from the Wreckin' Cru, and was not eager to do him any favors. In the end, Williams agreed to introduce Eazy to Heller, but not as a friend—he charged Eazy $750 for the introduction, which took place at Macola Records in March 1987.

Heller was a veteran of the music industry. He had managed groups as far back as Credence Clearwater Revival in the 1960s, and he introduced American audiences to U.K. stars Pink Floyd and Elton John. Heller was ready to retire from the business when he heard about the scene at Macola. In their meeting at Macola, Eazy told Heller about the kind of company he wanted Ruthless to be, and he played two songs: "Boyz N Tha Hood" and the first song recorded by N.W.A., called "Straight Outta Compton."

HOW THE DOCTOR OPERATES—THE MAKING OF *STRAIGHT OUTTA COMPTON*

Dre introduces the album *Straight Outta Compton* with the foreboding intonation that listeners are about to witness the "strength of street knowledge," a fitting opening statement from one of the most influential artists in hip-hop music.

Dre built the title track to N.W.A.'s *Straight Outta Compton* on a drum break from the Winstons, a Washington, DC, funk band. Dre sampled the drum break from their song "Amen Brother," a funky version of a joyous church hymn. In contrast to the high-tempo, disco-flavored tracks Dre produced with the World Class Wreckin' Cru, "Straight Outta Compton" has a slower pace with fewer beats per minute, creating a feel better suited to a convertible rolling down a California highway than a discothèque.

Dre boosted the bass on the kick drum and added an incessant high-hat that gave the beat shades of a high-tech, relentless urban tension. Using a Roland 808 synthesizer, Dre added the deep bass drops that gave the song an aggressive rumble. Dre used turntables to scratch in samples of euphoric exhortations "Yeah! Huh!" along with a snare drum and a droning, siren-like horn line that spiced up the beat even more.

Like most other hip-hop DJs making original songs, Dre composed by piecing together snippets of songs, gathering material from albums of all styles and spanning decades of recorded music. As hip-hop scholar Jeff Chang points out, Dre was unique in that he also brought live musicians into the studio to contribute to his tracks. On "Straight Outta Compton," Dre brought in guitarist Stan "the Guitar Man" Jones for a funky staccato riff that bolsters the track's musicality. Dre and DJ Yella used turntables to add percussive noises, and they mixed the sounds of machine-gun fire into breaks between raps.

With the first three tracks on *Straight Outta Compton*—the title song, along with "Fuck Tha Police" and "Gangsta, Gangsta"—Dre drew the blueprint for West Coast gangsta rap. Later tracks on *Straight Outta Compton* harkened back to Dre's disco days, and indeed Dre and N.W.A. bandmate the Arabian Prince produced similar dance-floor-fillers for other artists like J. J. Fad, Michel'le, Cli-N-Tel, and the Sleeze Boyz. But, as Chang notes, these pop acts sounded like "relics of an age of innocence" that *Straight Outta Compton* slammed the door on forever. "Nobody would be dancing anymore" (Chang, 2005, p. 319).

"WHO'S GOING TO BUY THIS CRAP?"

Heller says that when he heard the music and listened to Eazy describe his vision for N.W.A., he got the same feeling as when he first discovered Pink Floyd or Elton John. "It blew me away," says Heller. "I thought it was the most important music I had ever heard" (McDermott, 2002, p. 17). Eazy and Heller agreed to work together. Heller sent the band on tour and started calling record company executives, looking for a partner to help promote and distribute N.W.A. The band's first tour was hardly glamorous. For most of the gigs, they shared the bill with a female party rap trio named Salt-N-Pepa who had scored national hits in the 1980s with party songs like "Push It." While Salt-N-Pepa flew from show to show, N.W.A. had to drive themselves. The girls reportedly found it quite amusing that these self-styled "gangstas" were puttering along the tour in a van.

Meanwhile, Heller had little luck trying to sell the group to record industry executives, who often expressed utter disbelief that anyone would pay money to hear N.W.A. Heller, however, had some good reasons for his faith in N.W.A. "Boyz N Tha Hood" had already become an underground hit in L.A., but nobody suspected the extent to which the song had filtered out of Compton and into the larger hip-hop world. The song's popularity became clear when Heller took Eazy to New York to introduce him to important figures in the music industry. They were riding on an elevator at the Park Lane Hotel when the elevator stopped and Joseph Simmons and Darryl McDaniels, the front men for Run-DMC, got on. When the two rap heavyweights figured out that this suspicious-looking kid was Eazy-E of N.W.A., they began softly rapping the lyrics to "Boyz N Tha Hood." The record was a 12-inch single sold out of Eazy's car at Los Angeles swap meets—it had never been played on the radio anywhere—and yet here were two of the biggest stars in rap singing every word.

To capitalize on the success of "Boyz," Macola compiled that song and a handful of demos and rough recordings that various people had done for Ruthless and released the record as *N.W.A. and the Posse*. Only three songs were performed by what would become N.W.A., and the record didn't sell well, but it did bolster N.W.A.'s reputation as word of their new style spread without any help from the music industry or the press. One of the first people to catch on was Johnny Phillips—nephew of Sam Phillips, the man who discovered Elvis Presley—who worked as a record distributor in Memphis. Phillips heard about N.W.A. from one of his accounts, a record store owner in Cincinnati who had heard that the new group was getting played in local clubs. The store owner bought several hundred copies of the record from Macola, and found that they sold immediately. Within a month, Phillips was ordering several thousand copies.

Phillips worked as a distributor for Priority Records, a new company in Los Angeles created by Bryan Turner and Mark Cerami, former executives at K-Tel Records. Just two years old in 1988, Priority produced a line of rap compilation albums, and they scored an unexpected hit with an album of soul oldies recorded by the California Raisins. The Raisins were four animated raisins, voiced by black singers, who starred in a popular television commercial singing Marvin Gaye's classic "I Heard It through the Grapevine." The Raisins' album sold two million copies for Priority, which left the company brimming with cash and looking for new talent in which to invest. Coincidentally, Priority's offices were on the same floor of

Chapter 4

THE WORLD'S MOST DANGEROUS GROUP

N.W.A.'s *Straight Outta Compton* was Dre's first real try at producing the important hip-hop album he dreamed of making. Years later, after Dre had released *The Chronic* (1992) and *Doggystyle* (1993), two of the most important hip-hop albums ever made, he would express embarrassment over the simplicity of the production quality on *Straight Outta Compton*. Nevertheless, the record was a stunning success, and N.W.A.'s debut album is now seen as one of the most important records in the history of American popular music. At the time, however, N.W.A.'s success was hardly a foregone conclusion.

A NEW WAY OF DOING BUSINESS

Dre always felt confident he could make hit records, and the underground success of early N.W.A. releases encouraged his outlook. Now, with Ruthless Records aligned with Priority, Dre had fellow believers with deep pockets.

From a business point of view, hard-core rap seemed like a good risk. When N.W.A. went into the recording studio to make their first album, the record business typically spent $100,000 to make an album, and it was not unheard of for some albums to cost $1,000,000 or more. Once the record was produced, companies spent millions more marketing and promoting the record—creating a "buzz" around artists and encouraging radio stations to play the music. With this kind of investment required to make an artist into a popular star, most record executives were disinclined to take risks on new artists.

One of hip-hop's innovations was to upend this big-money system. Hip-hop artists like Dre could make an album with little more than a drum machine, turntables, and a sampler—something many kids could afford with an after-school job. Dre made *Straight Outta Compton* in about six weeks, at a cost of about $8,000.

In the case of N.W.A., their explicit lyrics were also seen by executives as a way to control costs. After all, it was obvious that no radio station would play anything from N.W.A., so Priority executives didn't need to spend money trying to convince the stations otherwise. N.W.A. was, in an odd way, a safe bet. Priority's Bryan Turner estimated that the company could make money if N.W.A. sold as few as 50,000 or 60,000 records. Seeing the possibility of profit with little up-front investment, Priority could afford to sign N.W.A. and then leave the group alone to make whatever type of music they wanted. Priority's gamble paid off.

NIGGAZ WITH ATTITUDE

Priority released *N.W.A. and the Posse* in 1987, followed by Eazy-E's solo debut, *Eazy-Duz-It.* Both were essentially party records, and nothing about them caused the critics to sit up and take notice. No one was prepared, however, for what would happen with the release of N.W.A.'s album debut, *Straight Outta Compton* in 1988.

The album sounds loose, as if the boys were working quickly and having one heck of a good time doing it—everybody, that is, except for Ice Cube, who wrote many of the album's most ferocious and socially conscious lyrics. Dre and Yella shared production credits on the album. The two DJs were usually the first ones to arrive at the studio and the last ones to leave, as the rappers came and went.

There was never any question, however, that Dre was in charge. "Dre was like the main ear," says Ren. "He'd tell you, 'Try to make it like this.' You'd do it. He'd be like, 'Cool.' Or 'That's terrible.' Dre'd look at you like, you dumb mother ... " (McDermott, 2002, p. 17).

Straight Outta Compton's album cover is a photo of the group standing in a semicircle, staring down at the camera. To the viewer, it looks as if you've been surrounded by a street gang, and you're staring down the barrel of a handgun Eazy-E is pointing in your face (quite a change for Dre from the white, shiny outfit he wore in his album photos with the Wreckin' Cru). The music is no less confrontational.

REAL GANGSTAS

Fans and critics have described *Straight Outta Compton* variously as politically subversive genius, a wake-up call to white society from black

America or, more often, as un-listenable, morally bankrupt garbage. It is all of those things.

The fifth word on the first song of the album is unfit for polite society—that word, and many different forms of it, appear perhaps hundreds of times on *Straight Outta Compton*. The record is full of the language and imagery of the small-time street hoods that N.W.A. wrote about, a viewpoint that many people did not understand. Almost immediately, the record prompted cries for censorship. N.W.A.'s concern for those people and their opinions was obvious—they didn't give a damn, and they said it loudly. That, for N.W.A., was the joy. In fact, it was not so much the language of N.W.A. that shocked people, but how much fun they seemed to be having while saying it.

As Cheo Hodari Coker pointed out in his writing on N.W.A., the group represented a more nihilistic viewpoint than the New York City rappers who were at the time considered "hard-core." The lyrics of rappers like KRS-One and Public Enemy's Chuck D were often overtly political, generally advocating black unity to resist the oppression of white society. When KRS-One displayed an automatic weapon on the cover of his *Criminal Minded* album, he still seemed like a rapper doing it all for show. "Ice Cube was different," writes Coker. "He sounded like a gangster, the hardest one rap and street life had ever produced. A man who had serious beef with the world and your place in it, and if you got in his way, you were getting capped" (Light, 1999, p. 258).

Yet Coker asserts that for all N.W.A.'s rejection of conventional "black power" themes, the group "epitomized the spirit of the Black Panthers," which had its roots in Los Angeles. Dre's "street knowledge" spoke to oppressed people who were sick of playing by white society's rules and ready to pick up the gun, as advocated by Panther founders Huey P. Newton and Bobby Seale.

Although it is true that the lyrics reflect harsh realities of Compton street life, it is also important to remember that the band members were not actual gang members. "It's just an image," says MC Ren. "We got to do something that would distinguish ourselves. We was just trying to be different" (McDermott, 2002, p. 30). For people who knew the members of N.W.A., particularly Dr. Dre during his stint with the World Class Wreckin' Cru, the new gangsta image came as a surprise. Longtime L.A. rapper King Tee, one of the pioneers of West Coast gangsta rap, said that N.W.A. seemed like a drastic departure from Dre's days with the Wreckin' Cru: "It's like damn, these niggas is the ruffest gangsta rappers around and they used to sing like Prince and shit" (Cross, 1993, p. 219).

Real gang members responded to the music with ambivalence. On one hand, the music was extremely popular among many actual gang members—indeed, it was the raps that real gang members performed on street corners and in prison yards that inspired N.W.A.—but some gang members did not appreciate the way N.W.A. had incorporated the gangsta image to make money, without actually walking in the dangerous shoes of a real gang member. Hip-hop scholar Eithne Quinn quotes a gang member named OG Tweedy Bud Loc articulating the resentments: "I'm fed up with the busters [hustlers] like N.W.A. A lot of my homies in the neighborhood died, man, and what the niggas did was market our life and our image. All them niggas in N.W.A. is buster! They never give back to the neighborhood" (Quinn, 2005, p. 83). This confusion between what is real and what is pretend is an important feature of gangsta rap. As we will see in upcoming chapters, sometimes the inability for listeners, critics, and the artists themselves to distinguish between the fantasy of gangsta rap and the reality of the life it reflected had important consequences for Dre and many others involved in "gangsta" rap.

GANGSTA GOES SUBURBAN

Even without the benefit of radio or television airplay, sales of *Straight Outta Compton* climbed into the hundreds of thousands in 1989.

For one thing, N.W.A. appeared at a time when African American listeners were getting tired of the polished pop of artists like Michael Jackson and Prince. Young African Americans wanted to hear music that more accurately reflected the tensions and aggression they experienced growing up in neighborhoods that in the 1980s were feeling the effects of decades of subtle and not-so-subtle racism from city officials (as discussed in chapter 2) and national economic troubles that seemed to hit black people especially hard. Life was not the party it appeared to be in pop music. Life was rough, and people wanted a music that expressed that reality. "After a while, Michael Jackson didn't work," says Doug Young, an African American record promoter. "People didn't believe the hype. We didn't care. We didn't feel it, with all that trying to be shy nonsense. People weren't checking for that no more. Rap made it gritty" (*Welcome to Death Row*, 2001).

Six months after its release in late 1988, *Straight Outta Compton* was an underground success. As expected, radio wouldn't touch it. N.W.A. taped a video for "Straight Outta Compton," but MTV refused to air it. Slowly, however, sales began to climb. *Straight Outta Compton* basically sold itself.

Johnny Phillips, the Memphis record store distributor, says small, black-owned record stores form unique relationships with their customers.

"Black customers in particular will buy where they can trust the store," says Phillips. "Doesn't matter what it is. We've sold to combination record store/barber shops, even a pet store/record store" (McDermott, 2002, p. 31). Those relationships were critical to getting N.W.A. distributed nationally, even when no mainstream outlets would touch the record.

N.W.A. spread nationwide, one region at a time. Once the N.W.A. record had appeared in a particular part of America, it crossed over into the white markets almost immediately. Soon, kids in suburban junior high schools saw that the N.W.A. record had the illicit air of forbidden fruit. After that, the biggest problem for Priority was keeping the record in stock.

In July 1989, *Straight Outta Compton* had sold nearly one million records when the venerable rock magazine *Rolling Stone* picked up on the N.W.A. phenomenon. Describing the record as a "harsh hip-hop documentary of L.A. ghetto life that includes gangbangs, drive-by shootings and police sweeps," reporter Steve Hochman conducted the interview in Ice Cube's bedroom "at his parents' very suburban-looking home in the notorious south-central part of L.A.," where, Hochman noted, he "hardly seems a threat to civilization" (Hochman, 1989, p. 24).

Although still in their early twenties, the members of N.W.A. seem precociously savvy about how they could use the media to play up their threatening image. As usual, Dre shunned the reporter, leaving the rappers Ice Cube and MC Ren to do the talking. "We don't want to go around telling people 'Don't do drugs,' or preaching safe sex, 'cause everybody's going to do what they want regardless." As white listeners bought *Straight Outta Compton* by the truckload, Cube proclaimed that his goal was to teach suburban teens something about ghetto life. "We told the truth on this record, so now we're going to teach the truth. Now we got a bigger audience that buys our records and likes us but don't really understand. We're gonna show them the raw reality of life. When they come out the other end, they gonna say 'Damn, it's like that? For real?' And we're gonna make money. Those are the goals" (Hochman, 1989, p. 24).

Indeed, N.W.A. would never have become so popular without support from white listeners who supported aggressive bands from both rock and hip-hop genres in the late 1980s. In a *Rolling Stone* column called "Music's Mean Season," critic Anthony DeCurtis noted that the end of the 1980s saw the rising popularity of unusually violent and angry bands like N.W.A. as well as hard rock acts like Guns 'n' Roses: "Nineteen eighty-nine was a tough year for anyone who still clings to the belief that rock & roll is inherently liberating, a joyful noise rife with 'the magic that can free your soul'" (DeCurtis, 1989, p. 15).

What was it about N.W.A. and Guns 'n' Roses that captured the attention of young white Americans? "They like listening to that 'I don't give a fuck' attitude," says Eazy-E, who often noted that the same people who bought Guns 'n' Roses albums also bought gangsta rap (Cross, 1993, p. 201). By the summer of 1989, it wasn't just white rock fans and major music magazines that had caught on to N.W.A. The federal government had taken notice, too.

THE FBI GIVES N.W.A. A BOOST

Straight Outta Compton might not have received so much attention had it not been for the controversy surrounding the second song, "Fuck Tha Police." The song begins with a courtroom scene, with Dr. Dre playing a judge presiding over a trial that pits N.W.A. against the Los Angeles Police Department. Ice Cube plays prosecuting attorney, and Dre asks him to "take the muthafuckin' stand … and tell everybody what the fuck you got to say." Cube launches into a profane tirade against police who "think they have the authority to kill a minority." He reiterates complaints about police that would have been familiar to many of the young black men hanging out on the streets of Compton: racial profiling and unprovoked brutality, for which Cube promises a "bloodbath of cops dying in L.A."

Although Cube's lyrics on *Straight Outta Compton* are now hailed as social criticism because they gave a nationwide voice to the rage felt by many low-income African American men, it is not true that N.W.A. was a "political group." Most of the songs on *Straight Outta Compton* consist of Dre's dance mixes and silly lyrics. The most overtly topical song, "Fuck Tha Police" almost didn't make it on the record. In interviews, Cube says that when he showed Dre the lyrics, Dre first responded with indifference.

That changed when police caught Dre and Eazy shooting paint balls at people at Torrance bus stops. That incident apparently caused Dre to change his mind and put the song on the record. This decision paid off, ironically, when the Federal Bureau of Investigation heard about "Fuck Tha Police."

N.W.A.'s reputation among teenage listeners as a surefire way to shock their parents was bolstered by the highly publicized opposition to "Fuck Tha Police." In August 1989, Priority Records received a letter from Milt Ahlerich, Assistant Director of Public Affiars for the Federal Bureau of Investigation. Following is the text of that letter:

> A song recorded by the rap group N.W.A. on their album entitled "Straight Outta Compton" encourages violence against and

disrespect for the law enforcement officer and has been brought to my attention. I understand your company recorded and distributed this album, and I am writing to share my thoughts with you.

Advocating violence and assault is wrong, and we in the law enforcement community take exception to such action. Violent crime, a major problem in our country, reached an unprecedented high in 1988. Seventy-eight law enforcement officers were feloniously slain in the line of duty during 1988, four more than in 1987. Law enforcement officers dedicate their lives to the protection of our citizens, and recordings such as the one from N.W.A. are both discouraging and degrading to these brave, dedicated officers.

Music plays a significant role in our society, and I wanted you to be aware of the FBI's position relative to this song and its message. I believe my views reflect the opinion of the entire law enforcement community.

Sincerely yours,
Milt Ahlerich
Assistant Director
Office of Public Affairs

(Chang, 2005, p. 325)

Priority executive Bryan Turner says the letter frightened him. "I showed it to some lawyers. They said [the FBI] couldn't do anything. That made me feel better. Then we circulated the letter. The thing was like a nuclear explosion. Once we circulated that, everybody wanted to hear the record the FBI wanted to suppress" (McDermott, 2002, p. 31). When N.W.A. went on tour, they were banned from performing in some cities, where the group was sometimes greeted with small riots. N.W.A.'s tour promoters tried to secure a promise from the band that they would not perform the song, while the 200,000-member Fraternal Order of Police officially voted to boycott any group that advocated violence against law enforcement officers. At a concert in Detroit, local police showed up in huge numbers. The crowd chanted "fuck the police" all night, so the group decided to play the song. As soon as Ice Cube uttered the opening lyrics, police rushed the stage and the group fled.

Music critic Dave Marsh and N.W.A. publicist Phyllis Pollack broke the story about the FBI's letter in an article in New York's *The Village Voice* newspaper, and they organized the American Civil Liberties Union and music industry leaders to formally protest police censorship. Turner sent Ahlerich's letter to members of Congress, and the FBI backed off. As it turned out, Ahlerich and the FBI had written N.W.A. the best advertisement they could have asked for.

For savvy record executives, it was no surprise that N.W.A. hit big among young white listeners. It is simple to identify the elements of a hit record, says former rap label executive Bill Adler. "Pop music is teen music. The stuff that's going to explode are the things that appeal to teens," Adler says. "Girls want somebody cute. Boys want somebody tough" (McDermott, 2002, p. 31). For teenage boys looking for new ways to shock their parents, what better way to do it than playing a record condemned by the FBI? Shortly after that, "gangsta" culture became a topic of mainstream discussion in major magazines—even fashion magazines published spreads on gangsta style.

In a sign that N.W.A. had gone mainstream, MTV, which had previously shunned the group, devoted the entirety of their hour-long show *YO! MTV Raps* to N.W.A, on which the group brandished assault rifles and aimed them at the camera to play up their "gangsta" image. Because all the publicity came free, without investment from the record company, N.W.A. turned huge profits—Heller reported that if Priority sold 200,000 records, the company made a quarter of a million dollars. There were no longer any doubts among record executives that hip-hop was not a fad and that hard-core rap had huge market potential.

But the FBI's letter to N.W.A. also raised concern about government censorship of popular music. Barry Lynn, an attorney for the American Civil Liberties Union, asked the FBI to withdraw the letter, but the agency refused. "Here you have an intimidating letter sent because officials know that as a constitutional matter there's nothing else they can do," said Lynn. He continued,

> You cannot tell a record company that they can't sell rap music because it's insulting or offensive to some group. This song doesn't even come close to the advocacy of criminal activity, which would permit it to be regulated. I think the writer of the letter knows that, so he figures, "I can go to the record company and tell them how upset we are"—and, if not create the fear of God in them, at least the fear of the FBI's continued scrutiny. You don't like to know that government agencies

are conducting surveillance of what you do. It is a frightening experience. (DeCurtis, 1989, p. 16)

WHAT DOES "STRAIGHT OUTTA COMPTON" MEAN?

To music fans in 1989, it might have seemed that N.W.A. had exploded on the scene from out of nowhere. Music experts, however, saw that gangsta rap was simply continuing a tradition of California pop, with N.W.A. riding the fourth major trend in West Coast music: first, there was the surf and hot-rod music of the mid-1960s; then came the psychedelic rock explosion of the late 1960s, which was followed by the mellow country rock of the 1970s; and finally there arrived the gangsta rap of the late 1980s and 1990s. Seen together, these four disparate genres share the California influence—elements of car culture, drugs, rebellion, freedom, and the laid-back good life appear and reappear as common refrains.

For Dre, *Straight Outta Compton* was a first try at making a full hip-hop album, and so it hardly compares to his later work for Death Row Records, when he established the "G-Funk" sound on *The Chronic* and *Doggystyle*. As a producer, Dre had not yet found his voice with N.W.A.'s debut. Yet in the years since *Straight Outta Compton*, hip-hop music—and especially gangsta rap—has become a major force in the music industry, and music scholars and journalists have attempted to explain what the success of N.W.A. has meant for American culture.

In his history of the band for *Vibe* magazine, Cheo Hodari Coker begins with an extended meditation on N.W.A.'s use of the word "nigger." When Dre and Cube were teenagers, they heard comedian Richard Pryor use the word time and again on his comedy albums. But the notorious racial epithet had never been heard so many times on such a big-selling record.

For black people, Coker writes,

> *Nigger* resonates with malevolent power, the juxtaposition of hate and love, and gains its strength from the ugliness of white racism, and the beauty and grace that exists in spite of it all.... By exploiting the fear and freedom associated with this word, [N.W.A.] realized they could capitalize on America's secret fascination with its own pathology. From *King Kong* to *Jurassic Park*, the white public has always been in awe of huge, untamable forces of nature—even as they assure people that they have everything under control. (Light, 1999, p. 252)

Whereas supporters hailed N.W.A.'s debut as arguably one of the most critically acclaimed and historically significant albums of the time, Coker points out that critics say N.W.A. opened a Pandora's box that changed the tone of American culture. N.W.A. critics contend that the group "introduced real violence and death to a world where cartoon macho boasting was previously the norm. It began, they say, with kids calling themselves 'nigger'; it ended with white gang members in Nebraska corn-fields pledging allegiance to street corners they had never heard of, Eazy-E dying of AIDS, and the violent, bullet-ridden deaths of Tupac Shakur and the Notorious B.I.G." (Coker, 1999, p. 252). Of course, none of this was in the mind of N.W.A. as they recorded the record. "Too much was made of supposed political motivations and probably not enough of the fact that these were kids making records for other kids" (McDermott, 2002, p. 30).

In trying to understand why *Straight Outta Compton* enjoyed such great success while arousing such intense feelings, journalist Terry McDermott points out that, unlike the comedy of Richard Pryor, the music of N.W.A. may have seemed too "real." In interviews Dre often compared *Straight Outta Compton* to the popular Quentin Tarantino film *Pulp Fiction*, a dark comedy that is also extraordinarily violent and rife with the word "nig-ger." There were no attempts to ban the movie, however. All the sex and violence in N.W.A.'s lyrics were a big joke to Dre, and he never under-stood why so few listeners understood that.

"The difference is the level of respect accorded not to the artists but to the audience," says Alan Light, the founding editor of *Vibe* magazine. He points out that critics presume a movie audience can better tell the dif-ference between fact and fiction, whereas the hip-hop audience, presum-ably, cannot. Journalist Terry McDermott points out that *Straight Outta Compton* may have been so successful and affecting because N.W.A. dis-guised the fictional nature of their work too completely. It was all an act when Eazy-E showed up on MTV brandishing an assault rifle, but for some people it might have seemed too real (McDermott, 2002, p. 33).

Whatever the reason behind their appeal, N.W.A. transformed the fledgling rap music industry. For better or worse, N.W.A. redefined hip-hop at the exact moment when hip-hop music was on the verge of taking over popular culture. *Straight Outta Compton* provoked much debate within the hip-hop community itself. Hip-hop fans who had been influenced by the political liberation philosophies of their parents saw N.W.A. as coun-terproductive, even as they found themselves drawn to Dre's irresistible sound. Hip-hop fans recognized that young minorities were largely absent from popular culture, and this aggressive new music was accompanied by a wave of new black radio stations, magazines, clubs, and cafés. Some radio DJs and journalists were outraged by lines like "life ain't nothin' but bitches and money," so they denounced N.W.A.'s belligerent ignorance and called for a boycott. Yet progressive hip-hop fans denouncing N.W.A. found themselves with uncomfortable allies: the Christian right, the FBI, and demagogue politicians.

Writer Jeff Chang notes that many hip-hop fans who decried N.W.A. would later come to have an "N.W.A. moment," such as the one recounted by journalist Sheena Lester, formerly an outspoken critic of the group. "I was going to a club ... and I remember being in the middle of the dance floor, hearing 'Dopeman' for the first time and stopping," she said. "The lyrics just struck me so tough I had to step to the side and really concentrate on what they were talking about. And that's when I fell in love with N.W.A." (Chang, 2005, p. 328).

At a time when pop culture was the only culture that mattered, *Straight Outta Compton* delivered hard-core hip-hop deep into the recesses of mainstream America—not bad for Dre's first try at making a record.

Chapter 5

GOING TO NUMBER ONE

Straight Outta Compton brought N.W.A. almost instant success. Dre's street-wise production, Cube's fiery lyrics, and the controversy that raged around the album combined to make N.W.A. an important group almost overnight. By the turn of the decade, America had embraced gangsta rap with characteristic ambivalence. Even as critics condemned N.W.A. for promoting violence, the Grammy Awards and *Billboard* magazine added categories for rap. Rap clothes were being sold in malls across the country; there were rap movies, rap comedy shows, rap video shows, and rap commercials. Even the Pillsbury Doughboy, a classic symbol of wholesomeness, had a rap.

Yet anyone even slightly aware of rock and roll history could recognize that N.W.A.'s rocket ride to fame wouldn't be without trouble. The story of a band's disintegration under the hot lights of fame is a common tale, so it seemed obvious that the volatile cocktail of personalities in N.W.A. couldn't last without trouble.

DRE THE HIT-MAKER

The success of *Straight Outta Compton* left Ruthless Records flush with cash and looking to sign new acts. Dre worked as the house producer at Ruthless. His musical vision gave Ruthless a distinct sound, and by the turn of the decade, journalists were already noticing and identifying a sound that was uniquely Dre's—edgy beats supporting loose, funny, violent rapping. Journalists noted Dr. Dre's expanding sphere of influence and remarked that by 1990 Dre's style had been appropriated by "an astonishing number of other rap producers" (Gold, 1990, p. F6).

HOW DOES HE DO IT?

By 1990, Dre had produced a stable of hit artists for Ruthless Records. *Straight Outta Compton* went platinum, as did the record Dre produced for Eazy-E, *Eazy Duz It*. N.W.A. intended their music to be heard as reflections of the stories and language they heard on the streets of Compton, but the ribald, cartoonish tales on *Eazy Duz It* reinforced the idea that gangsta rap is also supposed to be taken as a joke. "N.W.A. is nasty and hard-core," said Dre. "N.W.A. is about what the kids in Compton are feeling. That's how they feel about the cops. That's why they can relate to that song. We didn't make this stuff up. It's right there. Get any kid in Compton and put a mike in his hand and tell him to rap. What you'll get is the same kind of stuff as on the N.W.A. album. Eazy tells funny stories and makes you laugh," said Dre (Hunt, 1989, p. 76).

Dre produced other records as well, such as the single "We're All in the Same Gang," an antiviolence song in which most of California's most popular rappers perform a verse. The single was an interesting reminder of the way the record industry seemed to understand that the gangsta image portrayed a negative image to impressionable listeners, but the rappers must perform intricate verbal contortions to denounce violence while maintaining their street credibility. The verse performed by Ren and Dre is particularly confusing, suggesting that the only reason for their listeners not to kill each other is to keep "a smile off a white face."

In black music the producer is the most important creative force behind the songs, comparable to the role a songwriter plays in crafting hits in Nashville country music. Superstar producers include Bumps Blackwell, Sam Phillips (who produced Elvis Presley and Johnny Cash), Phil Spector (who made some of the greatest albums by the Beatles), Motown's Holland-Dozier-Holland, the Gamble and Huff team of Philadelphia, and Quincy Jones (Michael Jackson's producer). As Dre's work at Ruthless produced a string of hits, critics were starting to add Dre to that list of greats.

Dre is notoriously aloof and reserved in public, offering very few details about his personal life. He is an enigma. The question many journalists seem to want to know is, "How does he do it?" How is it that having Dre as a producer can virtually guarantee a hit record?

"Versatility is my middle name," said Dre, noting the success of Ruthless in the late 1980s. On one end of the spectrum was the violent hard-core rap of N.W.A. At the other end of the spectrum was J. J. Fad, a female trio with clean-cut raps about love and romance. Eazy-E's solo albums were comical (the humor was often intentional, but not always—Eazy was a great businessman, but not a particularly talented rapper or lyricist). There was also a singer named Michel'le, who became Dre's girlfriend. "I wanted to try something a little different. Her album has a rap feel. The songs have rap music tracks—the kind you'd hear on a rap album—but Michel'le is doing vocals, not a rap. A lot of radio stations won't play rap but would play a song with vocals that has a rap feel" (Hunt, 1989, p. 76).

The best rapper at Ruthless was the D.O.C., whose raps had a street edge without much profanity. Dre discovered him in Texas. "I liked the fact that he has a tight delivery and a strong voice," said Dre. "He was raw, but I was sure he could be shaped into a good rapper" (Hunt, 1989, p. 76). He had a hit record with his debut album, *No One Can Do It Better*, and his career appeared promising until a freak automobile accident crushed his vocal chords and left him unable to rap. Whether Dre was in the studio with a gifted rapper who just needed a little instruction or some guy off the street who had never sung a note, Dre boasted he could make a hit out of anybody.

"I don't know what I do, I just do it," said Dre. "It's instinct. It's feel…. It's judgment … A lot of it is very spontaneous. A lot of D.O.C.'s album was done on the spot in the studio" (Hunt, 1989, p. 76). Dre says that one of his greatest satisfactions is spotting an unknown artists with raw talent and shaping him into a pop artist. "Everybody who walks has something he or she can do in the studio," Dre said, continuing,

> Every person walking has some kind of talent that they can get on tape. I can take anybody who reads this magazine and make a hit record on him. You don't have to rap. You can do anything. You can go into the studio and talk. I can take a fuckin' 3-year-old and make a hit record on him. God has blessed me with this gift.
>
> Sometimes it feels good for me to be able to mold an artist and get him a hit record and to show him something that was inside of him that he didn't know about. It feels good to me. Everybody in the business has called me to try and do some tracks, but I can't see myself doing anything for somebody who already has money, you know. (Gold, 1993, p. 124)

As a producer, Dre says his best asset is his discerning ear. "I have an ear for what's authentic, for what people will like. For street rap, it has to sound real, like the kids were overhearing somebody talk on the street. A lot of rap is phony—talking about stuff people don't care about and talking about it in a way that doesn't sound real. Our stuff is hip because it's real. The fans can tell right away" (Hunt, 1989, p. 76).

This fixation on authenticity is a hallmark of Dre's generation, young people saturated with advertisements, deeply skeptical of consumer culture, and ambivalent about their role as consumers in society. In the early 1990s, young music fans wanted to hear music that was art, not bland, inoffensive tunes written by corporate hit-makers trying to calculate the "next big thing." They wanted something that sounded like the honest expression of a real person with a point of view. Authenticity was not only a concern of rap—it was also the central preoccupation for fans of independent rock that, like hard-core rap, would become commercially successful (packaged as "grunge"). For Dre, his concerns with authenticity related to his connection to the streets of Compton, a place that his music had done much to define in the imaginations of many people who had never before heard of the place.

"I'm from the streets. That's important," said Dre. "I know what street rap sounds like. I've lived it. I stay in touch with it. N.W.A. is about what the kids in Compton are feeling" (Hunt, 1989, p. 76).

Dre's music celebrated a mythologized gang life in Compton, California, the teenage fantasies of a boy growing up idolizing gang members. The realities of living day-to-day wore on Dre, however. Once, while driving with Michel'le, his Mercedes was stolen at gunpoint in Inglewood. Even as he celebrated an idealized street life, he recognized that it was not a good way to live. "I've had enough of that kind of stuff. Living in these dangerous places gets to you. You have to get out to keep your sanity. The peaceful life is nice" (Hunt, 1989, p. 78).

MONEY PROBLEMS AND THE BREAKUP OF N.W.A.

Of course, the good times could not last. Ice Cube was the first to discover that all was not right with N.W.A. At the height of the group's popularity in 1989, when the tour hit Phoenix, Arizona, Cube stopped the show. Pat Charbonet—then-publicist for Priority Records and Cube's future manager—had been asking Cube some questions about his finances. How much money had Cube been making off the songs he had written for *Straight Outta Compton?* Where was the money, and when would Cube get it in his pockets? Cube didn't have any answers, so he stopped the group dead in its tracks.

At Eazy's request, N.W.A. manager Jerry Heller flew to Phoenix with new contracts in hand and $75,000 for each member who signed. The rest of N.W.A. eagerly complied, but not Cube. He told Heller he wanted a lawyer to review the contract. Although the others in the group ridiculed Cube for turning down so much money, Cube discovered that he did, in fact, have good cause to feel he was getting ripped off. According to *Rolling Stone* magazine, N.W.A. grossed $650,000 for their 1989 tour, but Cube received only $23,000, while Heller kept $130,000 for himself. By the end of the year, *Straight Outta Compton* and *Eazy Duz It* had sold a combined three million copies. Although Cube had written or cowritten about half the songs on both albums, he earned a total of $32,000 (Sager, 1990, p. 166). The former friends now stood in conflict. Cube left the group and California; he moved to New York to work with Public Enemy and their group, the Bomb Squad.

The departure of their most gifted lyricist was a problem for N.W.A. Dre could still be counted on to produce hit music, but now it was up to MC Ren and N.W.A. associate D.O.C. to take over the writing duties. Cube, for his part, kicked off a solo career with the release of *AmeriKKKa's Most Wanted* in June 1990. Compared to Dre's raw, sparse production on *Straight Outta Compton*, Cube's solo album was complex and rich, full of complicated samples, voices, and sound effects all backing up Cube's aggressive vocal tone. With the follow-up, *Kill at Will* in 1991, Cube put forward more mature lyrics that cast him as the grown-up gangbanger looking with remorse at his wild past.

Music journalists were eager to play up the hard feelings between the former N.W.A. bandmates, and both sides seemed eager to comply—they had clearly learned from the success of *Straight Outta Compton* that there is no such thing as bad publicity, especially for gangsta rappers. People were wondering whether Cube's success meant he had "defeated" N.W.A., even as groups associated with the two artists (a group called Above the Law, protégés of N.W.A. signed to Priority Records, and Cube's group Da Lench Mob) engaged in violent brawls in Anaheim, California, and New York City. In 1990 a *Rolling Stone* article describe a scene where Above the Law caught Cube alone backstage at a show at Anaheim's Celebrity Theater. The group ganged up on Cube before going onstage, punching him until Cube escaped.

N.W.A. KEEPS RUNNIN'

In fall 1990, N.W.A. released a five-song EP called *100 Miles and Runnin.'* On this record, Dre established himself as the master of West Coast rap with a production job that surpassed his work on *Straight Outta Compton* by leaps and bounds. Dre employed the Bomb Squad's technique of heavily layering samples and sound effects, but he used even funkier drum breaks and beats that "hit the bloodstream like … an adrenaline shot," according to one reviewer (Coker, 1999, p. 261). Without Cube, the group lost what political edge it had, but the lyrics remained as violent, misogynist, controversial, and popular as ever. Dre's skill in the studio made Dre rich and famous, but bad behavior outside the studio put his name in the media just as often, no doubt adding to the gangsta image that helped sell records.

During an interview for *Pump It Up,* a hip-hop show broadcast on the Fox Network, host Dee Barnes asked N.W.A. members about their relationship with Ice Cube. Yella poured an ice cube from his drink and crushed it on the ground. The show's producers juxtaposed that image with footage of Ice Cube boasting and smirking, saying he had the group "one hundred miles and running." Dre took offense, and he retaliated when he saw Barnes at a party for the group Bytches with Problems on January 27, 1991. According to a lawsuit filed by Barnes, Dre picked her up and "began slamming her face and the right side of her body repeatedly against a wall near the stairway" as his bodyguard held off the crowd. After Dre tried to throw her down the stairs and failed, he began kicking her in the ribs and hands. She escaped and ran into the women's restroom. Dre followed her and "grabbed her from behind by the hair and proceeded to punch her in the back of the head" (Light, 1991, p. 66). Finally, Dre and his bodyguards fled the building. Of course, N.W.A. didn't try to hide the incident. They celebrated it.

"Man, the bitch deserved it," Ren told *Rolling Stone* (Light, 1991, p. 66).

Dre himself told the magazine: "People talk all this shit, but you know, somebody fucks with me and I'm gonna fuck with them. I just did it, you know. Ain't nothing you can do now by talking about it. Besides, it ain't no big thing. I just threw her through a door" (Light, 1991, p. 66).

Barnes filed charges in February, and on August 27, Dre pleaded no contest to misdemeanor battery. He was ordered to pay a fine of $2,513, perform 240 hours of community service, donate $1,000 to the California Victims Restitution Fund, and produce a public service announcement denouncing domestic violence.

Barnes also filed a civil suit against Dre alleging assault and battery, inflection of emotional distress, and defamation. "Their whole philosophy has been that they're just telling stories, just reporting how it is on the streets," said Barnes. "But they've stared believing this whole fantasy, getting caught up in their press, and they think they're invincible. They think they're living their songs." Barnes told *Rolling Stone* that she continued to receive threats from associates of the band and that it took her several months to publicize her story because "it really messed her up" (Light, 1991, p. 66).

Dre, however, says that the real reason Barnes delayed her civil suit for several months is because she was trying to blackmail Dre into making albums for her. According to Dre, "So she calls me and says ... 'I'm gonna get you, you do some records for me and I'll forget about it.' I called her a week later, her manager says we want you to do four songs for Dee Barnes's album *Body and Soul* without your name. I said okay and signed the contract. Then the N.W.A. album came out and went to No. 1; she called and said 'I want a million dollars.' I said fuck you, she said alright your ass is going to court" (Cross, 1993, p. 199).

SOUNDSCAN SENDS N.W.A. TO NUMBER 1

The EP *100 Miles and Runnin'* sold well for N.W.A., but it was not a hit on the scale of *Straight Outta Compton*, which ultimately peaked at number 37 on the *Billboard* charts. Cube's departure and the lackluster showing for their second release led some observers to wonder whether N.W.A. was no longer at the forefront of the fast-growing hip-hop industry.

In the meantime, however, a critical change had taken place. In the summer of 1991, just three weeks before N.W.A. planned to release its second full-length album, *Billboard* magazine began using a new system to compile its record sales. Called Soundscan, the technology used a computer system that tracked record sales using information from bar-code scanners at record stores. Before Soundscan, *Billboard* ranked records by using anecdotal reports from record shop owners and radio programmers. The information was often skewed toward artists with the biggest marketing and promotion budgets and against underground artists like N.W.A. Although Soundscan still underreported sales from mom-and-pop record stores, it was certainly a more objective way to rank records. The results shocked the industry.

The album was called *Efil4zaggin* ("Niggaz 4 Life" spelled backward). Released in mid-summer 1991, the album entered the *Billboard* chart at number 2, the highest debut since Michael Jackson's album *Bad* in 1987. It was released without a single and with no video on MTV—there was not a single song on the album suitable for radio airplay. A week later, the album hit number 1; more than a million people bought *Efil4zaggin* in only two weeks.

As if to illustrate the unpredictability that the new Soundscan system introduced in the *Billboard* charts, the hard rock band Skid Row knocked N.W.A. out of their top spot just a week later. *Efil4zaggin* was the best-selling album for only a few days, but it reinforced the hip-hop revolution that N.W.A. had begun with *Straight Outta Compton*. The results forced the entire music industry—and, indeed, anyone with an interest in American culture—to rethink their assumptions about what would and would not sell in the American cultural marketplace. With the release of *Efil4zaggin*, a pattern emerged—a gangsta album is released; parents' groups, politicians, and critics push each other aside to denounce its content; and teenagers buy the album by the millions. It was a dubious landmark when the album was completely banned in the United Kingdom. N.W.A. had achieved a feat that not even the notorious punk band the Sex Pistols—long deemed the epitome of rock repulsiveness—ever accomplished.

However, a feud was brewing among the band that would eventually catapult Dre to even higher levels of stardom and controversy. The final disintegration of N.W.A. came about as the result of—what else?—money.

N.W.A. RUNS OUT OF AMMO

The story of Dre's departure from N.W.A. is the subject of much rumor and speculation. Working from court documents filed by Eazy-E in the aftermath of the breakup, *Vibe* magazine writer Cheo Hodari Coker provided a vivid account of what supposedly took place.

As N.W.A. was about to release *Elif4zaggin*, all seemed well with the group. Dre, Eazy-E, and manager Jerry Heller all owned multimillion-dollar homes in the same neighborhood in Calabasas, California. They led the fast-paced, hedonistic life accorded to major rock stars. Nevertheless, Dre, like Ice Cube, came to feel that he was not making as much money from N.W.A. as his artistic contribution warranted, and he accused Heller and Eazy of bleeding him dry.

"The split came when Jerry Heller got involved," Dre said later in an interview with *Vibe*. "He played the divide-and-conquer game. He picked one nigga to take care of instead of taking care of everybody, and that was Eazy. And Eazy was like, 'I'm taken care of, so fuck it'" (Coker, 1993, p. 262).

In April 1991, Dre arranged to meet Eazy-E at the Hollywood recording studio where N.W.A. was putting the finishing touches on *Efil4zaggin*. Eazy sat in the darkened studio, expecting Dre to show up. Instead, the man who walked into the room was a 6-foot, 320-pound Marion "Suge" Knight, a former college football star, bodyguard, and artist manager.

After a standout career at the University of Nevada–Las Vegas, Knight had played professional football briefly before beginning work as a bodyguard for hip-hop stars. Dre and Knight had met through Priority

Records rapper the D.O.C., whom Knight had visited in the hospital after the rapper suffered the serious car accident that ended his career, and nearly his life. Dismayed at the lack of care the D.O.C. seemed to be receiving, Knight had investigated Priority to find out how much money the D.O.C. was making on his records.

"D.O.C. sold his publishing to Jerry Heller for a watch and a chain. Jerry had the words 'watch and chain' right there in the contract. I ain't never seen no shit like that in my life," Knight told *The Source* magazine (Coker, 1993, p. 251). Dre was growing suspicious of Eazy and Heller, so he asked Knight to look into his financial situation as well.

Dre wanted Eazy to release him from his contract with Ruthless Records. Eazy refused. The impasse led to what reportedly transpired between Eazy and Knight at the studio in 1991.

"You gonna sign the release?" Knight asked, presenting Eazy with papers that would free Dre, D.O.C., Above the Law, Kokane, and Michel'le of their obligations to work for Eazy and Heller. Eazy refused.

Knight reportedly declared that he had kidnapped Heller and was holding him prisoner in a van. Eazy continued to resist. Then Suge allegedly produced a piece of scrap paper and showed it to Eazy. It was his mother's address. "I know where your mama stays," said Suge, as several muscular men brandishing lead pipes appeared behind him. Finally, Eazy gave in and signed the releases (Coker, 1993, p. 262). N.W.A. was dead. Dre and Knight would stick together to create Death Row Records, for which Dre would produce more groundbreaking hip-hop albums that marked the further evolution of gangsta rap.

THE AFTERMATH OF N.W.A.

The members of N.W.A. went on to do very different things after the group came to an end.

Antoine "DJ Yella" Carraby remained marginally involved in music, helping produce tracks for a 1994 release by a rap group called Bone Thugs-N-Harmony, and Yella released his own solo album, *One Mo Nigga to Go*, in 1996. Since then, Yella has apparently retired from music and now films pornographic movies.

After Ice Cube left the group, he fell into a feud with the rest of N.W.A. On the title track for the album *100 Miles and Runnin'*, Dre refers to Cube as a "bitch" in one of his raps, and the group insults Cube by his real name, O'Shea, on the song "Alwayz into Somethin'." On the album *Elif4zaggin*, they call Cube "Benedict Arnold," an infamous traitor who betrayed an American fort to British soldiers during the Revolutionary War.

The insults apparently hurt Cube. His debut album *AmeriKKKa's Most Wanted* (1990) didn't mention N.W.A. at all. He appeared in the major motion picture *Boyz N the Hood* (named after N.W.A.'s first song), and in that movie there is a scene where a petty thief wearing a "We Want Eazy" sweatshirt gets beaten. On his next album, *Death Certificate* (1991), Cube took on N.W.A. in his lyrics. He called the group "phonies" and derided Eazy-E as a "snitch." He also made remarks about N.W.A. manager Jerry Heller that some considered anti-Semitic, saying Eazy "let a Jew break up my crew." In 1992, Ice Cube toured America on the bill of the popular Lollapallooza music festival, which brought rock and rap acts together and helped Cube widen his fan base. Also that year, he converted to the Nation of Islam, a sociopolitical organization with the stated purpose of uniting black Americans and improving their conditions. In 1992 he released his most popular album, *The Predator*, which sold more than two million copies; however, his audience began to decline as albums from Dr. Dre and Snoop Dogg captured the attention of hip-hop fans. Even so, critics consider his 1992 collaboration with Da Lench Mob on the album *Guerillas in tha Mist* as an artistic triumph. That year, he also married his current wife, Kim.

In 1993, Cube reunited with Dr. Dre for a duet on the song "Natural Born Killaz," which appeared on the soundtrack to the *Murder Was the Case*, a 19-minute film/music video. But even as Cube reconciled with Dre, he became involved in verbal feuds with a host of other rappers and groups such as Cypress Hill and Chicago rapper Common—which went so far that after exchanging increasingly tense insults in song, Cube and Common met with Nation of Islam leader Louis Farrakhan to reconcile their differences.

In the mid-1990s, Cube embarked on what would become a successful film career, beginning with the hit *Friday*, a 1995 comedy starring Chris Tucker. Also in 1995, he starred in *Higher Learning*, a film by writer and director John Singleton, who also directed *Boyz N the Hood*. In 1996, Cube formed the group Westside Connection with fellow rappers Mack 10 and WC; their debut album *Bow Down* was a critical success, with the song of the same name reaching number 21 on the singles charts. Cube released a long-awaited solo album, *War and Peace Volume 1* in 1997; *War and Peace Volume 2* (2000) featured a reunion with Dre and fellow N.W.A. rapper MC Ren. Ice Cube continues to make records and appear in major films.

The career of Eazy-E after N.W.A. is a sad story. After Dre left N.W.A., Eazy released a string of albums: *5150 Home 4 Tha Sick* (1992), *It's On (Dr. Dre) 187Um Killa* (1993), and *Str8 Off tha Streetz of Muthaphukkin Compton* (1995). The album *It's On* sold more than two million copies, and, as the title suggests, it spends a good deal of time dissing Dr. Dre in response to the insults Dre had directed at Eazy-E on Dre's 1992 album, *The Chronic*. Eazy's album even includes pictures of Dre from his days in the Wreckin' Cru, wearing the lacey outfits and makeup.

In 1993, Eazy-E entered a hospital with what he believed to be bronchitis. However, he was diagnosed with the sexually transmitted disease Acquired Immune Deficiency Syndrome, otherwise known as AIDS. Eazy, who fathered seven children with six different women, is believed to have contracted the disease through unprotected sexual activity. This came at a time when AIDS was largely associated with gay men and carried a heavy stigma, especially in the hip-hop community. One month after Eazy announced he had AIDS, he died on March 26, 1993, at Cedars-Sinai Medical Center in Los Angeles at the age of 31. His battle with the disease emphasized the point that AIDS was not merely a threat to gay men. Dre visited Eazy in the hospital, and although those two men are the only ones who know what they said to each other, it seems that they put their feud to rest. On Dre's 1999 album *2001*, Dre directed a rap to Eazy, indicating that their beef was water under the bridge and that Dre missed his old friend.

Chapter 6

RAP AND RAGE:
LOS ANGELES AFTER N.W.A.

The albums *Straight Outta Compton* and *Efil4zaggin'* introduced the world to the music Dre had envisioned ever since he was a teenager crafting songs in his Compton bedroom. With funky beats and dark comedy, gangsta rap became the dominant style of hip-hop at a time when hip-hop was about to become the loudest voice of American youth culture.

Dre's craftsmanship on *Efil4zaggin'* proved that gangsta rap could be delivered with catchy hooks and interesting musicianship, which helped make gangsta rap a viable commercial product. Until Dre released *The Chronic* in 1992, *Efil4zaggin'* stood as the best gangsta rap record ever produced, and when it hit number 1, there were few record executives who remained unconvinced of gangsta rap's lucrative potential. With N.W.A., Dre attained fame, fortune, and credibility as one of hip-hop's most talented hit-makers.

Efil4zaggin' illustrated gangsta's massive appeal while, at the same time, showcasing gangsta's limitations as well. As Cheo Hodari Coker noted, "Unless they carried a redemptive message, gangsta rap records, even the best ones, are all about the same things: getting high, awaiting death, looking to kill enemies, self-loathing, fucking and not trusting so-called bitches, and keeping a watchful eye on one's monetary dealings. If you're only painting with three colors and using the same canvas over and over, how can you not repeat yourself to death?" (Light, 1999, p. 262).

N.W.A. opened the door for a legion of gangsta rappers endlessly repeating the themes of the genre that N.W.A. had established. At a time when new digital technology began to allow large corporations the ability to transmit electronic media—television, music, movies, Internet web pages—on an unprecedented scale to young Americans with equally unprecedented amounts of disposable income, gangsta rap touched off a debate about what, exactly, young people were buying into.

Is gangsta rap an uncensored report from black America? Does the music glorify and perpetuate violence? What responsibility do artists and record companies bear as a result of their creation and marketing of such provocative material? As we will see in later chapters, such questions have undergone endless debate since N.W.A.'s debut. Clear answers have been elusive, but hip-hop scholar Jeff Chang, in his book *Can't Stop, Won't Stop*, provides an illuminating context for N.W.A. in America that helps frame a thoughtful discussion of gangsta rap and the nature of Dr. Dre's contribution to American culture.

WHERE YOU FROM?

With his relentless celebration of Compton, Dre turned the focus of hip-hop, which had always been a deeply local, homegrown art form, ever more deeply on urban geography. What Chang calls the new "hood-centric" aesthetic emerged at a time when inner-city neighborhoods were forced to be more self-reliant after large federal budget cuts during the 1980s. The federal government shifted a greater portion of the costs for urban infrastructure—roads, public schools, social services, and so on—to state and local governments. The effect of this shift was that suburban areas, with high property tax revenues and low numbers of residents living below the poverty line, fared well. Urban areas, with fewer affluent residents and larger budgets for police and social services, declined. More than ever, life in America largely depended on where you were from.

Meanwhile, evolving technology made it relatively cheap to produce a hip-hop record. With no more than a pen and paper, a microphone, a mixer, and a sampler, kids could make their own gangsta rap tapes. Small companies like Ruthless Records could produce sophisticated, great-sounding records with little help from major companies. N.W.A.'s rapid success showed just how easy it was for determined young rappers to bring their story of life in their neighborhood to an audience of millions.

RAP AND RAGE IN LOS ANGELES

The dual plague of drugs and gangs rose up together in Los Angeles, with gang activity growing more violent as the cocaine trade became more profitable.

In 1988, Los Angeles police chief Darryl Gates declared a "War on Gangs," with City Hall approving an increase of 650 officers to bring the force to its largest size ever. The effort resulted in 25,000 arrests, sometimes as many as 1,500 in a day (most of the youth were released with no charges, although their names were recorded in police databases). The program was not a success. Many hard-core gangsters got tipped off about police raids and escaped arrest. In 1992 the department paid out $11 million in brutality settlements and spent only $2 million on gang intervention programs. N.W.A. did indeed give voice to the growing frustration that African Americans felt in a climate of fear and hostility in their neighborhoods.

In hindsight, N.W.A.'s gangsta rap could be seen as a warning that there was a bomb of pent-up rage waiting to blow up in South Central Los Angeles. Race and crime made good headlines for local media, and tensions grew. In March 1991, a videotape appeared that lit the fuse.

On Sunday, March 3, an amateur's camcorder captured five Los Angeles police officers beating Rodney King at the entrance to Hansen Dam Park in Lakeview Terrace. King was drunk and had led police on a chase that ended in the park. The video, broadcast nationwide on cable news channels, showed King cowering beneath a ring of officers swinging batons and kicking—during a minute and a half, King received 56 blows, stomps, and kicks to the head and body.

With gang homicides at a record high and tensions in Los Angeles also reaching a zenith, gang leaders moved to broker a truce among the web of various groups stemming from the city's two main gangs, the Crips and the Bloods. During a series of delicate peace meetings in spring 1991, gang leaders drafted an agreement based on a 1949 United Nations treaty that created a temporary cease-fire between Israel and Egypt. The so-called "Multi-Peace Treaty" committed both parties to end drive-bys and random shooting to promote "the return of Black businesses, economic development and advancement of educational programs." It included a gangster code of conduct that encouraged family life, civic participation, and education; that discouraged alcohol and drug abuse; and that stood against using "the N-word and B-word." Gang leaders signed the treaty on April 26, 1991. Two days later, 250 Crips and Bloods marched to city hall for a formal presentation of the truce to the Los Angeles City Council. A peace party was underway when news of the Rodney King verdict hit the streets and obscured their good intentions.

On April 29, after a week's deliberation, a jury returned verdicts of "not guilty" in the charges of assault against the officers who beat Rodney King. The news broke at 3:15, and less than an hour later, black youth began attacking Korean-owned liquor stores. (In 1991 there were three times more liquor stores in South Central Los Angeles than in the entire state of Rhode Island, and long-lingering animosity existed between African Americans and Asian Americans.) Anyone who was not black and who was unlucky enough to pass by the intersection of Florence and Normandie on April 29 was attacked. Unrest spread to other street corners as mobs set fires, turned over cars, smashed windows, and threw rocks. The streets were jammed with groups chanting "No justice, no peace" and cars blaring "Fuck Tha Police," a sign of how N.W.A. had served to both predict and fuel actual violence. By the end of the day, the riot had claimed 14 lives.

Police established a perimeter around South Central as the inner city deteriorated into war-zone conditions—rioting, arson, and looting, with Korean storeowners barricaded in their stores firing warning shots at would-be thieves. The Los Angeles riots ended on May 1, when the National Guard posted tanks in South Central. The final statistics were shocking—53 dead, mostly from gunfire. More than 2,380 people were wounded, and property damage reached $1 billion.

President George H. W. Bush told a television audience that what they saw in Los Angeles "was not about civil rights. It's not about the great cause of equality that all Americans must uphold. It's not a message of protest. It's been the brutality of a mob, pure and simple. And let me assure you, I will use whatever force is necessary to restore order" (Chang, 2005, p. 378). King appeared on television looking unbearably sad, begging, "Can we all get along?" (Chang, 2005, p. 376).

The riots also put gangsta rap under more scrutiny than ever before. As Chang notes, "these days would mark the hip-hop generation's passage through fire. After this, there would be backlash" (Chang, 2005, p. 379).

GANGSTA IN THE SPOTLIGHT

The years after N.W.A. appeared saw a surge in official concern over the content of rap music, and the rhetoric was amplified as politicians headed into the presidential election season of 1992, which pitted Democrat Bill Clinton against Republican George H. W. Bush and third-party candidate H. Ross Perot, a Texas billionaire.

The controversies were many. The Miami rap group 2 Live Crew saw their album *As Nasty as They Wanna Be* banned as obscene by a Florida judge, although in May 1992 an Atlanta federal appeals court overturned the decision. Meanwhile, Los Angeles rapper Ice-T prompted police outrage with his heavy metal–rap hybrid song "Cop Killer," which he recorded with his band Body Count. Democratic candidate Bill Clinton engaged in a war of words with rapper Sister Souljah, who told the *Washington Post*, "I mean, if Black people kill Black people every day, why not have a week and kill white people?" (Chang, 2005, p. 394). Souljah was commenting on the hypocrisy she perceived in a white government that seemed to ignore the real problem of inner-city conditions and black-on-black murder, yet vehemently denounced rap albums that talked about killing police.

After scrambling to catch up to gangsta rap after the success of N.W.A., major-label companies were now trying to sell off controversial gangsta artists as political pressure mounted.

Meanwhile, the gang truce persisted and encouraged a flourishing creative scene for hip-hop in Los Angeles. Rappers like DJ Quik, Compton's Most Wanted, and Above the Law put hits on the chart. An underground scene of freestyle rap, spoken word, free jazz, dancing, and graffiti art emerged at sites such as the Good Life Café, Leimert Park, and Hancock Park. Such magazines as *URB* and *Rap Pages* captured the local scene. In an interview with a *Rolling Stone* reporter, Dre, with his characteristic ambiguity, dismissed the furor over gangsta rap as so much media hype, even as the hype he denounced boosted his record sales:

> Dre: People are always telling me my records are violent, that they say bad things about women, but those are the topics they bring up themselves. . . . This is the stuff they want to write about. They don't want to talk about the good shit because that doesn't interest them, and it's not going to interest their readers. A lot of the motherfuckers in the media are big hypocrites, you know what I'm saying? If I'm promoting violence, they're promoting it just as much as I am by focusing on it in the article. That really bugs me out—you know, if it weren't going on, I couldn't talk about it. I mean, you will never hear me rapping about Martians coming down and killing motherfuckers, because it's not happening. And who came up with that term *gangsta rap* anyway?
>
> Reporter: Dre, you did.
>
> Dre: Oh, maybe so. Never mind then. (Gold, 1993, p. 124)

As the popularity of gangsta rap skyrocketed in the 1990s, so did the career of rapper and producer Dr. Dre. Courtesy of Photofest.

Dr. Dre and Snoop Doggy Dogg appear in Rolling Stone's *"'93: The Year in Review" issue, December 14, 1993. Courtesy of Fox/Photofest.*

Dr. Dre, considered a hip-hop pioneer, created gangsta rap by blending the sounds of 1970s funk and soul with intense beats and gritty lyrics. Courtesy of Photofest.

Eminem, pictured here in 2000, is one of Dr. Dre's most significant protégés. Courtesy of Interscope Records/Photofest.

Dr. Dre appears in the film Training Day *(2001), directed by Antoine Fuqua. Courtesy of Warner Bros./Photofest.*

Chapter 7

WELCOME TO DEATH ROW

As Dre was solidifying his separation from Eazy-E and Ruthless Records, Suge Knight was busily planning his future in entertainment, having started his own label with sports agent Tom Kline, a man he'd previously protected while still a bodyguard. They called the new venture Funky Enough Records, a name meant as homage to one of the D.O.C.'s songs. They set up shop in Kline's Beverly Hills office, and Kline received part of the company in return. Knight soon signed popular West Coast hip-hop artists Chocolate and DJ Quik both to the label and to his management, a setup largely unheard of in the music industry. Although Knight didn't offer a salary, he did give the artists plane tickets home, a place to stay, and food while they worked on tracks.

Knight quickly won the loyalty of both Chocolate and DJ Quik because he was one of them, having come up in the 'hood, on the same streets of Compton. And as a music executive, Knight didn't succumb to the pressure to "cross over" into white audiences by softening rap's hard edge. Because of groups like N.W.A., rap had become a multimillion-dollar industry, and the pressure to appeal to wider audiences was becoming overwhelming. Knight promised his artists not only that he would let them make truly black music from the streets, but also that they would be paid for it.

Ironically, though, it was the success of a watered-down white rapper that ended up funding what would later become Death Row Records.

VANILLA ICE

In 1990, a year after Chocolate signed to Knight's label and management, Dallas rapper Vanilla Ice, legally known as Robert Van Winkle, quickly rose up the *Billboard* charts with his hit "Ice, Ice Baby," an easy rap set over the classic Queen-and-David Bowie song "Under Pressure."

A handful of white rappers had already worked their way to mainstream success, with the most respected being New York's Beastie Boys. The group, around since 1979, originally started as a punk band, morphing to a hip-hop group under the thumb of Rick Rubin. Their 1986 release *Licensed to Ill* was the first rap album to reach number 1 on the *Billboard* album charts, where it reigned for a then-record five weeks. It also hit number 2 on the urban album charts. The album became the best-selling rap album of 1980s.

In early 1990, Ice seemingly came out of nowhere, equipped with a ready-made "from the streets" background.

But as Vanilla Ice's background proved to be largely contrived, so was his ability as a songwriter. Chocolate had written the popular song a few years back for Ice's little-known debut album, *Hooked*. Vanilla Ice's manager Tommy Kwon had commissioned Chocolate to author some tracks after the Dallas club owner had seen both Chocolate and his partner DJ Earthquake perform.

At the time, Chocolate said, Kwon promised to pay the pair for their work on the album. Without management, Chocolate accepted the verbal contract.

Chocolate told Knight about his gentleman's agreement with Kwon, adding that Ice would likely need more songs for a follow-up album, assuming his first album was successful.

Almost instantly, Knight contacted Kwon and Ice, who called Chocolate, asking him to come to Texas to work on his follow-up article.

Chocolate immediately left, bringing with him R&B singer Paradise, who was also under Knight's management. At Dallas's Hard Rock Cafe, Chocolate handed over a cassette of new songs to Ice.

But as Vanilla Ice's *To the Extreme* climbed the charts, Chocolate still could barely afford to eat because the only compensation he'd received were shared songwriting credits on the album. Chocolate wanted publishing rights, which would grant him payment every time the song was played on the radio, covered, or performed live. On a top-selling album like *To the Extreme*, these rights could easily be worth several million dollars.

"Only two people worked on that album, Earthquake and me," Chocolate said. "I don't know why everybody else got credit, including Vanilla. Only thing he did was learn the songs and rap. He didn't do no production. Didn't do shit.

"Vanilla was no writer or creator on the record at all. And he got paid more than anybody!" (Ro, 1998, p. 36).

Knight, who recently had been released from Los Angeles County Jail on an assault charge, promised Chocolate he would handle his situation. Knight then employed intimidation tactics similar to those that got Dre and the D.O.C. released from Ruthless, tactics that would soon become his trademark.

"The first time I met Suge Knight was at a restaurant in L.A. called Palm.... And I was sitting there, eating a nice meal, and all of a sudden these huge guys—it looked like a football team—showed up," Ice said in a televised interview several years later. According to Ice, Knight simply stared at him, asking, "How you doing?"

Knight repeated this brand of intimidation several times, including during an incident that left Ice running from a restaurant, screaming that gangs were after him.

In a 1996 interview with television's *PrimeTime Live*, Vanilla Ice claimed that Suge came to his Los Angeles hotel room with an entourage of thugs who quickly "outpowered and outnumbered" Ice's bodyguards. Ice, a tall, skinny man, said he was physically frightened of the 6-foot, 3-inch-tall Knight.

Knight then asked Ice to join him on the balcony, where Ice claimed that Suge first asked him to look over the side, noting the 15-story height. Ice reported that Knight then grabbed his feet and flipped him, holding him over the edge of the balcony, threatening to let go if full publishing rights to seven songs on *To the Extreme* were not signed over then. Ice agreed, signing papers that Knight promptly provided.

"I signed them and walked away alive," Vanilla Ice said in the *Prime-Time* interview.

In a later interview, Ice recanted the balcony story, claiming Knight never used violence to coerce his signing away the publishing rights. It did, however, take an order from a court for Ice to finally pay Chocolate what he now says Ice owed him.

Knight received 25 percent of the money earned by publishing rights on his album.

"You can look at it like I was an investor in Death Row Records with no return on my money," Ice said in the *PrimeTime* interview.

The promise of money for Knight came at the perfect time. Knight's partner Tom Kline decided to back out of the deal with Knight, kicking Funky Enough out of its Beverly Hills office. But as the label began to fold, Knight met Dick Griffey, an icon of the black entertainment industry.

SOLAR AND THE FORMATION OF DEATH ROW RECORDS

Griffey ran SOLAR, or Sound of Los Angeles Recording, a popular 1970s label born from an alliance of Griffey, an attorney, and Don Cornelius, the famed host of *Soul Train*. Together the pair signed and produced such popular acts as Shalamar and the Whispers, producing hits both stateside and in England.

Music promoter Wes Crockett, whom Knight once protected as a bodyguard, introduced Knight to Griffey. Griffey listened to Knight's vision for a label, and offered Knight both studio and office space in his building downtown.

Griffey, impressed by Knight's business prowess, realized that the new-found music executive would likely find gold in his newest partner, Dr. Dre.

According to a 1989 deal, Dre would produce a set amount of albums with Ruthless Records that Sony would then distribute to stores. SOLAR held a similar deal with Sony, though Dre did not work on their albums. But once Knight's label was in-house, Griffey told Sony that Dre would now be working through SOLAR and that Sony should contact him if they wanted Dre to produce anything.

They did. They wanted him to produce the soundtrack to the upcoming movie *Deep Cover*. The movie, set with an urban background, showed an undercover cop getting in too deep. Sony wanted its soundtrack to be gritty. Griffey told Sony that Dre would need money, given that Ruthless had cut off most of Dre's income. Sony offered $1 million dollars to Dre for his music publishing rights, as well as offering to draft the necessary releases from Ruthless for Dre to perform.

"I was there when Dre said he sold his soul to the devil for a million bucks," Griffey said. "And I swear, the devil's got to have a receipt for his ass."

It was then that Dre asked Eazy up to the SOLAR building for a meeting. Eazy arrived without security, and unarmed, where he then signed the releases.

"It was like *The Godfather*," Ruthless attorney Michael Borbeau later said in an interview with reporter Ronin Ro. "Sony wanted Dre, who was a very hot producer, so they had releases drafted for Knight to bring to Eric Wright. They wanted him to sign the papers. And if he didn't sign the papers, he knew the consequences" (Ro, 1998, p. 54).

The releases were signed, and Sony was told they could go ahead with the *Deep Cover* soundtrack. Dre—along with almost all of the rest of Ruthless' rosters—was now with Knight.

Dre and Knight moved forward with their new label, calling it Futureshock, after a George Clinton song. Former Ruthless act Above the Law still had a Dre-produced album coming their way, though Dre said he'd have nothing to do with it unless they signed with Futureshock.

Eazy immediately retaliated by suing Sony, Dre, Knight, and SOLAR for unscrupulous business practices. But Sony claimed that Ruthless, which was to deliver three Dre-produced albums, didn't hold up their end of the deal. Dre had stopped working with Ruthless after he felt his pay was too low, and Eazy had used other producers on the albums. The albums Ruthless did release were commercial failures, leading Sony to claim that Ruthless releases without Dre were of a terrible quality. Because of this, Sony claimed, Ruthless was guilty of a breach of contract.

But Sony offered Ruthless, and Eazy, a deal. If they would let Above the Law record one song with Dre, a song that could be used on the *Deep Cover* soundtrack, they would call it even. Knight, then acting as Dre's manager, agreed with the deal. Eazy soon signed.

But despite this fairly amicable agreement, Ruthless and Eazy-E continued to warn Sony against working with Knight, filing RICO, or racketeering, charges against the companies. And though Sony realized Knight was necessary to get Dre to produce the *Deep Cover* soundtrack, Sony cut off almost all funding to the fledgling Futureshock label.

Those days, Knight largely bankrolled the label, relying on money earned though Chocolate's publishing rights and money saved while a bodyguard. Because Griffey housed the label in his building, Dre and Knight saved money on studio time, which is easily the greatest expense in making a record.

But Knight, Dre, and the D.O.C. wanted to own their own studio. Griffey soon offered to sell a floor of his building.

They themselves too poor to by the studio, they soon found a benefactor.

Michael Harris, known on the streets as Harry O, was a notorious drug kingpin, having set up shop in at least 11 states. Harris, connected to the Bloods, often worked directly with Columbian drug lords. But, like many who gain their money through illegal activities, Harris also funded other endeavors, including some in the entertainment industry.

As one of the first black men to have produced a play on Broadway, Harris produced *Checkmates*, which starred a then-unknown Denzel Washington. Harris was familiar with the entertainment industry, and despite being in prison, he was eager to return to entertainment, only this time with music.

"Mike Harris had a wonderful background in entertainment," said Norman Winter, former Death Row publicist, in the 2001 documentary

Welcome to Death Row. "[But] I thought he was an entrepreneur in New York. I had no idea he was in jail" (*Welcome to Death Row,* 2001).

Harris spent his days at the Metropolitan Detention Center in downtown L.A., incarcerated on several charges of drug trafficking and distribution.

"A young man by the name of Eric had told me about Suge's background, and that Suge was aware of my background, and that he was somewhat intrigued behind my past and he had wanted to hook up with me in some form or fashion," Harris said. "I made the hook-up and we talked on the phone a few times" (*Welcome to Death Row,* 2001).

Harris's lawyer, David Kenner, cleared the way for Knight to visit him in jail. Harris reportedly asked Knight what it would take to start this label. Knight told him that for approximately $1.5 million, the pair could be partners, with Dre and Knight splitting their half of the partnership. Harris told Knight that would be no problem; he would fund the label.

Harris and Knight agreed to name their new venture Death Row, under a parent company called Godfather Entertainment. Harris said he told both Kenner and Knight to put the business in their names. Dre and Knight would be equal partners, with Knight handling any administrative and managerial tasks while Dre ran the studio and produced albums. Kenner would represent Harris's interest in the company, along with Harris's wife, Lydia Harris.

In a 2006 *Monterey County Weekly* article, Lydia Harris said, "When we started Godfather Entertainment, Michael would always say, 'Lyd, make sure you always document everything—you know, keep records of everything.' And at the time I didn't know anything about anything, really, so I just followed his directions. What paperwork I didn't keep, David Kenner had on file for the company, as part of a good-faith agreement with us."

Not long after signing the incorporation contracts, though, Knight and Kenner filed separate papers for Death Row Records, ones that did not carry the Godfather Entertainment name. They did not tell Harris, who had already deposited money into the Death Row account.

With Harris's funding, their studio was soon carpeted, new speakers were installed, the artist received allowances, and some were given apartments.

At a cost somewhere between $35,000 and $50,000, Death Row officially debuted in February 1992 at a swank Beverly Hills club called Chasen's. Their invitation list was an entertainment-industry roster as hundreds of music executives from New York and Los Angeles were served with an invitation that read like a subpoena:

You are hereby ordered to appear before the honorable Dr. Dre and the officers of GF Entertainment, as a guest of the court, to witness the springing of Death Row Records.

Knight gave constant television interviews during the party, claiming the label as a home for neighborhood rappers and producers to prove themselves. Holding a glass of champagne, Knight proudly professed that he, along with Dre, had in no way forgotten where they came from, pledging allegiance to the streets from which they hailed.

The one paying the tab, though, was missing, still serving his time. Although Knight and Kenner openly thanked Harris for his funding initially, soon all mention of the man was scarce, with his presence almost exclusively limited to his regular calls from jail as well as his wife's occasional presence at the studio.

Even so, at the party, Kenner toasted Harris on camera, calling him by his street name Harry O, in what would be one of the only public references to the drug lord. The FBI soon seized the tape.

"When Death Row first started, they were big because they did stuff that nobody ever did," said Jerome "Muggs" Taylor, founder and president of I Funk Records, in the 2003 documentary *Dr. Dre: Attitude Surgeon.* "The record label executives carried guns. When they went to concerts and people ran up on the stage, they got kicked up off the stage. It was like hard core. It was Death Row. You're not coming with that, really street, for real. And that was the first label that really kept the gangsta … not watered down … not Hollywood."

Knight, ever the aspiring music executive, quickly stepped into his new role, running the company close to the imagery in the gangsta raps it produced.

The group kept true to these street roots, often committing the same acts of violence glorified in gangsta rap. Dre was arrested for breaking producer Damon Thomas's jaw after Thomas caught Dre leaving Thomas's girlfriend's house one morning. In New Orleans, Dre was arrested for attacking a police officer in a scuffle that ended with horse-mounted cops coming into the hotel lobby where Dre, Knight, and the D.O.C. were staying. There, Dre claimed, they were attacked by a group of men. The police came, though it was someone else who attacked the police, Dre claimed. A 15-year-old boy was stabbed during the riot.

"They [are] saying I beat up seven police and I incited a riot and some other shit," Dre said at the time. "I was like, 'Damn, that ain't saying much for your motherfucking police force if I beat up seven police'" (Ro, 1998, p. 84).

To Eazy, the increase in the violence surrounding Dre was directly attributable to Knight. Eazy commented,

> He [Dre] had that Dee Barnes thing, breaking that kid's jaw, driving his car off the cliff, getting shot, New Orleans. None of that shit ever happened to him when he was down with us. Dre's into something he can't get out of! Musically and personally. In every way. He's got people who don't know shit about the music business filling his head with bullshit, telling him he could be this and that, get "this and that"—fuck that! (Ro, 1998, p. 84)

Eazy wasn't the only one shaken by Dre's newfound violent tendencies. Sony was slated to release the album, an endeavor that also was to be a joint venture between SOLAR and Death Row. The deal would have marked a relatively unknown setup in the music industry: these men, most of whom were under 30, would have had the chance to get a distribution deal through a major label while keeping all the profits.

But Sony soon became wary of all the violence surrounding the label. Eazy still continued to insist that Dre, Knight, and Sony had wronged him. When Ruthless sued Sony for racketeering charges, Sony took *The Chronic* off its release list.

"People didn't want to take a chance on us, and it pissed me off," Dre said. "I mean, I had talent—talent that had already been proved with huge record sales from N.W.A. So you had to wonder what the fuck the problem was" (Ro, 1998 p. 92).

There were talks of a BMG distribution deal. Once executives at the major labels heard *The Chronic* lyrics, though, they refused to put out the album, which was almost completely finished.

Knight—and Dre—felt that no one was willing to risk distributing the album. Rappers were notorious for crime, said former *Hollywood Reporter* music editor Jeffrey Jolson-Colburn, in an interview in the documentary *Welcome to Death Row* (2001): "They go platinum; then they go to jail," he said.

INTERSCOPE RECORDS

Finally, though, in November 1992, Death Row found a label willing to take the chance on a group already known for its violence.

Headquartered in Los Angeles, Interscope records was a small new label run by Jimmy Iovine, an engineer who had worked with Bruce Springsteen and John Lennon. He partnered up with Ted Field, heir to the clothing retail giant Marshall Field; Field had already secured Interscope as a $30 million joint venture between Warner/Elektra/Atlantic and Field, who also had worked as a producer in Hollywood and was responsible for films such as *Three Men and a Baby* and *The Hand That Rocks the Cradle*.

Field hired Tom Whalley to head A&R, or artist recruitment, a position Whalley had held at Capitol Records. While at Capitol, Whalley had signed Crowded House and worked with Bonnie Raitt. At Interscope, he signed Tupac Shakur and Nine Inch Nails, two controversial acts with fairly robust sales. Despite this, though, Interscope financially struggled.

Soon, Warner/Elektra/Atlantic cancelled the contract with the label, and Interscope was out of money. Field, tired of personally funding Interscope, started looking for other deals, or at least a chance to turn a profit at the fledgling label. He soon met Dick Griffey, who handed him a copy of *The Chronic*.

Griffey, along with Virgil Roberts, had gone to the Interscope offices after a mutual friend recommended they approach Interscope. Iovine claimed to love *The Chronic* and offered to distribute the album as well as to supply an advance of $200,000. The money, though, didn't immediately come.

Griffey and Roberts waited, expecting a check to arrive. After several days, they finally received money, though only half of what they were originally promised, which was presented as a loan, not an advance. Both Griffey and Roberts claim that Jimmy Iovine then approached Knight and Dre, saying that Griffey had refused to make a deal with Interscope on *The Chronic*, and then offered the pair $1 million for the album.

Knight has publicly told a different story of how he and Dre came to work with Interscope. According to Knight, he and Dre did meet the Interscope executives at their Wilshire Boulevard offices. The three men had all known of Dre from his N.W.A. days and felt that he was an amazing producer, publicly claiming that everything the producer touched turned to gold.

But even so, Interscope didn't immediately jump at the chance to partner with Death Row.

"They didn't get it," Knight said at the time:

> They was sitting around the room, looking at each other, trying to figure it out. So we said, "Fuck it." I snatched the tape up and we left the meeting. When we came back, we had the entire album completed—artwork, video treatment, marketing plan, everything.

The guys in the corporate suits have so little respect for rap, they actually told me that Dre did not deserve to get the same amount of royalties they pay pop acts. I remember sitting there, trying to explain to those guys that Dre was as genius and that we were about to create this hugely successful record label, but they would just look at me like I was fucking crazy. (Ro, 1998, p. 95)

But Knight claims that just after Dre landed the cover of a November 1992 edition of *The Source*, with a .44 Smith and Wesson pointed at his head, negotiations with Interscope started again. Because Ruthless Records continued to insist that there was a breach of contract between them and Dre, Interscope was forced to pay both labels—Ruthless and Death Row—to agree that Interscope would distribute Dre's album *The Chronic* through Priority Records. The contract carried a clause: if Dre left Interscope, all of his legal and monetary rights as a producer and artist would go back to Ruthless.

This new deal sparked a separation between SOLAR and Death Row. Soon, Death Row relocated to Interscope's Wilshire Boulevard offices and cut all ties with Griffey. Griffey still maintains that both Dre and Knight were taken advantage of based solely on Knight's inexperience with contracts, publishing, and manufacturing.

"They ended up going to Interscope and getting one of those regular slave deals," Griffey said. "They took the kids away from the nest too soon" (*Welcome to Death Row*, 2001).

Chapter 8

THE G-FUNK ERA

A month before N.W.A's *Efil4zaggin* hit the streets in 1991, Dre threw a stag party at his house, inviting almost all his friends. There was a break in the music, and without much thought, Dre put a tape into the deck. It was a demo for his stepbrother Warren Griffin's group, 213, the name a nod to the area code of their hometown, Long Beach. The group also featured Nate Dogg and Snoop Doggy Dogg, a choirboy turned rapper whose laid-back style betrayed his clever rhymes.

Dre had heard similar tapes before. Although they were terrible in quality, Warren G. often passed along these demos to Dre, who always showed little interest in his project. But that day was different. Something about the rhymes grabbed him.

Once the tape finished, Dre reportedly hit rewind and played it again. Then again. And again. There was something about the way Snoop dropped the rhymes that drew the producer into the tape. Dre called his stepbrother and asked to talk to Snoop.

In the documentary *Welcome to Death Row*, Snoop recalled,

> Warren G. called me on a three-way and was like "Snoop, I got Dre on the phone, cuz. He liked the tape. He want to work with us, cuz." I'm like, "Nigga, stop lying." And he said hello. And I said, "Who this?" And he said, "This is Dre." He said, "That shit was dope." He said, "I want to get with you. Come to the studio Monday."

Snoop immediately told Nate Dogg that Dre was interested. Nate, a longtime Dre fan, jumped at the chance to meet the producer, later claiming he would have walked from Long Beach to Los Angeles if he hadn't had a car.

Once they met up, Dre asked Snoop to repeat his rhymes, and Dre liked his style even more than he had on the tape. Snoop's lazy way of delivering rhymes attracted Dre, whose production form was beginning to give way from the more hardened beats of N.W.A. to a more relaxed, melodic style now commonly called G-Funk, or gangsta funk.

G-funk is best characterized by its use of funk grooves and strong, me-thodic beats, a fierce style of rapping belied by slow, relaxed grooves, fe-male background vocals, and samples from 1970s funk songs.

Compared with the more socially conscious songs from groups like Public Enemy, West Coast G-Funk rappers mostly rhymed about women, drugs, and gang violence, themes introduced during Dre's N.W.A. days. The style dominated rap music for about four years, starting with the re-lease of *The Chronic* in December 1992 and ending when Dre left Death Row in 1996.

The sound was a sharp contrast to other albums emerging around that time, including those of Common and Wu Tang, Nas's *Illmatic*, and the Notorious B.I.G.'s debut *Ready to Die*, the album that established Sean "Puffy" Combs's Bad Boy Entertainment as a formidable player in the hip-hop arena.

Although the first traces of G-funk are found in N.W.A.'s "Alwayz into Something," almost everyone refers to the title song off the *Deep Cover* soundtrack as the G-funk's true starting point—and to Warren G. and Dre as the fathers of the style. The song "Deep Cover" not only solidified Dre's emancipation from Ruthless and Eazy-E, but also started Death Row Records and, arguably, Snoop's career.

SNOOP DOGGY DOGG

Snoop, born Calvin Broadus, worked as a bagger at a local grocery store while in school at Long Beach Polytechnic High School. Soon enough, though, the lure of the streets and the desire to be near friends in the Roll-ing 20 Crips, a local gang Snoop joined, soon had him selling dope out of his mother's home.

"I cut myself off from Snoop for two years when I found out he was selling drugs out of my house while I was at work. Putting him out was hard, but I had to do it as a mother and for personal safety," said Beverly Broadus, Snoop's mother, to *Rolling Stone* reporter Doug Wielenga at his 1995 murder trial (Wielenga, 1995, p. 22). "We had to watch our backs when we went to church, never knowing when someone might do a drive-by shooting."

Arrested at 18, Snoop served eight months in the Long Beach County Jail on a drug-related charge. A year after his release, he was back behind bars on a six-month sentence. Four months later, he served an additional four-month term when busted by undercover cops while trying to sell drugs to a local addict.

In jail, Snoop used his free hours to conjure rhymes, entertaining the other inmates with his easy flow and natural style. Seeing something unique in the young rapper, fellow inmates encouraged him to quit selling drugs and start rapping. He listened. Although he kept his connections with the Rolling 20 Crips, Snoop abandoned the outlaw life soon after his release.

Snoop recorded several demos, all on cassette, the background tracks scratchy from an old turntable with a damaged needle, in the hopes that friends from the Rolling 20s would like what they heard and help support the fledging rapper. No one did. He realized he needed some help. Snoop recruited Nate Dogg and Warren G., two musicians whose styles closely matched his own. The three had been friends since high school, making their collaboration natural. Warren being Dre's stepbrother was a twist of fate that worked well for the group.

After listening to that fateful demo, Dre immediately asked Snoop to work on the record with him, along with D.O.C. But the night Dre and Snoop met at the studio, the D.O.C. couldn't make it back in time to write lyrics for the title song that Dre wanted to start recording the next day. Dre knew how he wanted to song the start, but wasn't sure where it would go next, so he asked Snoop to help. Without a car, Snoop stayed at the studio that night. He worked on the song, writing lyrics within an hour. They recorded the song later that day.

"Deep Cover" not only introduced Dre as a solo artist, but also showed his ability to mentor others, with the artist mentored in this particular case being Snoop. Through "Deep Cover," Dre was able to bring a relatively unknown rapper to the forefront of hip-hop.

It was also in "Deep Cover" that Snoop uttered what would soon become his trademark phrase: "187 on an undercover cop." In California, this set of numbers is police radio code for murder.

The song peaked at number 166 on the Billboard 200 in July 1992, though the song also appeared on the charts a few other times when released on other albums, such as Dre's *First Round Knock Out* (2001) and Snoop's *Doggy Stuff and Doggy Style Hits* (2005). Fat Joe and Big Pun's 1998 single "Twinz" carried a sample from the song as well as the original chorus, dubbing it "Deep Cover '98." Snoop appeared in the music video. It also ranked number 4 on the *Billboard* rap charts.

Dre and Snoop also filmed a low-budget music video for the album, its story largely mimicking that of the movie: in his quest to implicate the bosses of an underground mafia, an undercover cop gets in too deep, becoming addicted to drugs while struggling to not blow his own cover.

The video opens with a smoky office, and Snoop, playing the role of the undercover cop, is with Dre and a large black man, who is seemingly the kingpin. The pair is initiating Snoop into the mafia, handing him a pipe filled with marijuana. Snoop has to decide whether to smoke the weed. The music starts, and with it comes a mix of images from the movie itself and black and white frames of Snoop and Dre embroiled in the gang life. In a dirty concrete bungalow, where a projector shows the movie on a wall while potheads lazily look on, drug squads raid the house.

The video did not receive widespread play on mainstream cable stations, though it sparked incredible interest in the song among the hip-hop community, an interest that exploded with the release of The Chronic.

THE CHRONIC

Released in 1992, Dre's first solo album, The Chronic has been hailed as a hip-hop masterpiece. A New York Times writer called it "the album that defined West Coast hip-hop":

> It's a hermetic sound, sealed off from the street noise as if behind the windows of a limousine or a jacked-up jeep; it's the sound of the player enjoying ill-gotten gains but always watching his back. With its mixture of clarity and deep bass punch, Dr. Dre's tracks jump out of ordinary car radios as well as boom boxes and fancy sound systems.

Not only did The Chronic bring to the mainstream the G-funk sound, but it also proved that gangsta rap could sell, with approximately five million albums sold. The album also introduced to global audiences the entire Death Row roster. RBX, Lady of Rage, Warren G., Nate Dogg, Dat Nigga Daz, Kurupt, and Snoop are all found throughout the album, having appeared on ten of the album's 16 songs and sketches and having been given songwriting credits on 13 songs.

Some of the lyrics from the album—most notably the introduction to the entire album—single out Eazy-E, Jerry Heller, and Ruthless Records. But Eazy, through the linked deal with Interscope and Priority Records, received between 25 and 50 cents per sold copy of the album, meaning he profited off a product that largely mocked him.

Undeniable even to Eazy was the appeal of the album, an appeal that even a natural critic couldn't resist.

"When George Clinton first heard hip-hop artists blending old records with new beats, he thought, 'Damn, that's pretty tacky,'" wrote one *Rolling Stone* writer. "Then Dr. Dre turned samples of Clinton's P-Funk sides into G-Funk, and Dr. Funkenstein approved, calling funk 'the DNA of hip-hop and rap'" (2003).

This marriage of styles demonstrated Dre's ability to produce an album far more widely accessible than any of the N.W.A. albums. The beat, largely danceable, played over familiar funk tunes as choruses chimed like that of rock songs' choruses. The rappers, or characters, as they were all acting a role—especially Snoop Doggy Dogg—were more likeable.

Although the subjects were largely the same as before, they now came across more playful—and less intimidating to a suburban white kid who, proving through purchase power that he liked his violence, seemed to prefer in an attractive, more melodic form. The reoccurring theme of marijuana and easy women—a placeholder in 1990s young white America—was more familiar than a police shoot-out in the gritty streets of Compton or the beating of a transvestite.

What Dre and the rest of the Death Row camp did was create something that no one else was producing at the time, their lyrics and style a fresh, more lighthearted approach to hip-hop when the more serious East Coast raps were dominating the industry. Listeners across the country, even the world, were invigorated by this new style that celebrated debauchery rather than contemplated complex social issues.

Soon, malls were packed with both black and white teens and young adults dressing in the baggy style of newfound heroes Dre and Snoop. Snoop, a relative unknown just a year before, suddenly found himself performing songs alongside Dre, the crowds singing along. He saw others who were not only dressed like him, but also styling their hair like him, mimicking his rap style in the influx of demo tapes that soon surfaced across Compton, Long Beach, and Los Angeles.

Across white America, the single "Nuthin but a 'G' Thang" resounded through the car windows of white suburban teens, and gang members from Compton to New York City bounced their heads to the beats of Dre. The song was a hit, and Death Row found a permanent home with success.

Singles from the album—"Let Me Ride," "Dre Day," and "Nuthin But a 'G' Thang"—all hit top spots on the *Billboard* charts, receiving repeated play on MTV and mainstream radio stations, two venues that had largely snubbed N.W.A. during its peak.

Videos for "Let Me Ride," "Nuthin' But a 'G' Thang," and "Dre Day" all feature a common format: Dre and Snoop rapping to the camera while spending the day hanging out, often at a barbeque or at a club. Album lyrics were changed to smooth down some of the explicit lines, though the common threads were still there. The songs sing like a Death Row roster, with shout-outs and appearances by Dre's Death Row label mates. Marijuana and murder, as well as the continued insults to Eazy-E, both started and filled out the rest of the album.

The album cover—which mimics the packaging of Zig-Zag rolling papers—solidified the reoccurring theme of the entire album: we smoke dope.

Even the name—*The Chronic*—refers to a more potent form of street weed as popular in the streets of Compton as it was the backwoods of Georgia. Dre and the rest of Death Row bragged in interviews how smoking marijuana helped create the album, though Dre claimed several times that the album name was chosen because the songs were dope, as opposed to being an extended commercial for dope.

The album has appeared on a variety of lists, including *Vibe*'s "100 Essential Albums of the 20th Century." It ranked number 137 on *Rolling Stone*'s list of 500 greatest albums of all time and was also included in *Rolling Stone*'s "Essential Recordings of the 90s"; it ranked eighth in *Spin*'s "90 Greatest Albums of the 90s" and sixth in *Vibe*'s "Top Ten Rap Albums of All Time."

The Chronic influenced countless imitators who have flooded the market, many of whom were on the Death Row label, with the style having become its trademark. Classic G-funk artists include Warren G., Tupac Shakur, Ice Cube, Paperboy, Kurupt, Nate Dogg, and RBX.

Says Jerome "Muggs" Taylor, founder of I-Funk Records,

> *The Chronic* changed the whole music game; people had to step their game up. Death Row—they took it the next level. It was here, and they bumped it up. It changed everything. They said, "Fuck that. This is how we are in L.A. We gang bang, we're hustlers, and we're going to talk about it." They were bumping Death Row and Dr. Dre records in New York, and that was unheard of. But Dr. Dre's *Chronic* album, it changed the whole game. It changed MTV, it changed BET, changed the radio—it just changed the whole country, even the world, universally. (*Dr. Dre: Attitude Surgeon*, 2003)

Chapter 9

THE MIDAS TOUCH

Almost as soon as it hit the streets, *The Chronic* proved to be a massive success, pulling in a more mainstream audience than N.W.A. had ever known. Two cable venues that had largely ignored gangsta rap until now—MTV and BET—played videos from the album in constant rotation. Images of Dre and Snoop at barbeques and house parties were projected into homes across the world as the album sold more copies than any other rap album at that point had.

Dre's lyrical glorification of the gangster life contributed to an atmosphere that not only allowed for violence but also celebrated it, much like in many N.W.A. releases.

Suburban teens who would never walk the streets of Compton were able to live out their gangster fantasies vicariously through Death Row artists and their music. And in cities that *were* like Compton, young black men and women saw and heard their daily lives portrayed through music videos and car stereos.

"The essence of the whole genre is the fact that it is our CNN; it is our *60 Minutes*; it is our *Dateline*," Michael Harris said. "Most artists try to be as factual as possible in depicting the actual experiences in our community" (*Welcome to Death Row*, 2001).

And when the experiences aren't necessarily there, such as for Dre and Knight, who had neither ever been in an actual gang, sometimes the image remakes the man.

Gangsta rap, once the anthem of the streets, was now a marketable commodity, one that Knight knew how to manipulate well through Death Row's close affiliation with street culture, and Dre worked perfectly from the mixing board.

According to Doug Young, former promoter at Death Row, in *Welcome to Death Row*,

> One of the things about these major labels is that they'll never understand street music, never understand stuff that starts right there in the neighborhoods, they'll never understand. Never will, never will, never will. That's why you will always have some young entrepreneurs who will come along, who really understand how to do that, and make a killing. (*Welcome to Death Row*, 2001)

Knight ran the label like a family, leading the group as he would a gang in the streets, using this mentality to generate interest often without overt advertising. As with many endeavors, word of mouth and personal endorsements often provided more credibility and increased sales than any advertising campaign. With Knight's direction, Dre's already solid street reputation, and the success of *The Chronic*, Death Row became incredibly popular among young black urban Americans. Performers regularly contacted the label, passing along demos and sometimes even waiting outside the studio doors, immediately performing upon seeing either Dre or Knight. The label seemed to understand these men, its leaders having struggled to enter the business themselves. This lent even more credibility to Death Row, resulting in a robust roster filled with young talent.

In interviews, Knight often claimed that, despite his newfound wealth, he was still from those Compton streets and had not succumbed to the Hollywood mindset. Death Row was still a label for the people, he'd often claim.

"Basically, they did the same thing Motown did," said former Motown executive Jonathon Clark in *Welcome to Death Row*. "They took the mindset, the spirit, the dreams, the hopes, and the thoughts of the people at the time and set it to music."

And those thoughts and dreams propelled Death Row to the top of its game, an odd feat in the music industry. This small company, run by young black men, hit at least double platinum with every release, something entirely unheard of in the music industry. Most industry executives are considered gifted when even 4 out of 10 releases hit platinum.

But even with these high record sales, many of the Death Row artists were still poor, with some resorting to the sort of street games they thought they had left behind once signed to a successful label.

"Even after *The Chronic* came out, I was broke and starving," rapper Nate Dogg said. "I used to sell dope to get gas money to go to SOLAR

Records to do *The Chronic* and *Doggystyle*. Wasn't nobody making money right then" (Ro, 1998, p. 107). Nate Dogg, like many on the Death Row roster, saw his songs appear on other albums that were most often considered a "collaboration." But, like the other artists, he fully expected his time to come and for Death Row to put out his album. Like the others, he waited out the poverty.

Knight often slept in the office, while Dre lived in a large house just outside of Los Angeles, in an affluent neighborhood. Meanwhile, many Death Row artists shared an apartment, including Snoop, who roomed with Daz and Lil' Malik, a young rapper who came out to California only to appear on Snoop's "Pump Pump" but then never went back to New York–based Rowdy Records.

"When Snoop was living in that apartment, he didn't have any furniture," said writer Brian Cross in an interview (Ro, 1998, p. 108). Even so, he kept faith that he would prevail in the music industry. "You're going to be the biggest thing to black people since the straightening comb," Dre reportedly said to Snoop.

To ease some of the stress, Dre often hosted parties at his house, most of which were filled with Death Row label mates and their bodyguards and small entourages. Still on house arrest for breaking producer Damon Thomas's jaw, Dre wasn't allowed to leave the house except for work, often hosting these parties after hours as his only means to socialize. But because he could use the label as an excuse to visit a club in the name of business, Dre still often found his way out on weekends. In the studio, the parties often continued. While recording *Doggystyle*, Snoop and Dre were kicked out of nine studios.

True to his methodical style, Dre produced *Doggystyle* in fits, spending hours at a time in the studio recording material he would likely discard.

"There's thirty-five or thirty-six reels of Snoop in there," Dre said during the recording of *Doggystyle*. "Each reel holds three songs. So far, I have five that I like. That's just a small example of how … how deep I'm going into this album. I feel that the tracks that I'm doing for him right now are the future of the funk." Dre continued, "I've never heard of the perfect album but I'd like to make one" (Ro, 1998, p. 111).

But his style created some tension in the studio as members of Tha Dogg Pound, and a few others, grew resentful of both Dre's production authority and his prominence in popular media. In the studio, Dre dictated the G-funk style. In articles, Dre was almost always depicted as the mastermind of Death Row.

Soon, Dre gave way to some pressure by Snoop to include others in *Doggystyle*'s production, speeding along the process. The second half of the album was recorded in about two days, the crew having drunk multiple bottles of Hennessy while laying down tracks. Dre, still under house arrest, hosted the crew at his place, where they worked for almost 48 hours straight.

Dre spent countless days reworking the material recorded that day. Snoop's cousin, on parole, drew the cover art. Once completed, Dre and Knight kept the album under tight wraps, hoping to avoid any bootlegging that might disrupt sales. But a man named Fabian "Fade" Duvernay, a promotions manager for Interscope, reportedly asked local club DJ Mark Love to play Tha Alcoholiks, a band Duvernay managed on the side, in exchange for receiving a copy of *Doggystyle* early. Knight overheard their conversation about the tape, and at work Monday, Knight told Duvernay he could either quit or get beat. Duvernay refused to quit, and as Knight began to beat Duvernay, a sole voice of reason asked Knight to stop. Soon, Duvernay began carrying a gun.

The debut party for the album, held on a boat docked at Marina del Ray and secured by Nation of Islam guards, was soon racked with tension. The guards were letting women in first, often separating them for their dates. Several of the hundreds of balloons decorating the vessel popped, causing people to duck because they thought it was gunfire. Finally, when Warren G. showed up with several of his Crips friends, a fight erupted with Knight's Blood buddies. Soon the police arrived, bringing with them helicopters, approximately 20 patrol cars, and the media. The party continued, though noticeably hampered.

Two days later, Knight invited the promoter responsible for the party to his office on the promise of more business. Once there, the promoter was locked in the closet where Knight and his men would allegedly beat down anyone Knight felt crossed him.

Warren G. almost immediately left the label, signing on at Def Jam. His first album with the New York–based label, *Regulate ... G Funk Era*, sold four million copies. Once on the market, *Doggystyle* sold 800,000 copies its first week and entered the *Billboard* charts at number 1. "When Snoop's album comes out, this is the most anticipated rap album in history," Griffey said.

Doggystyle was the first debut album to ever hit the top its first week, bringing in a surplus of money to Death Row. Artists who just months before had been selling drugs to get by now were earning high salaries, making the album's release akin to an early Christmas.

But as *Doggystyle* rose in popularity, the media depiction of Death Row worsened. Lyrics were dissected, and the rappers—mainly men—were depicted as real-life violent gangsters. Knight began to appear on the cover of magazines like *The Source*, and on more than one occasion, he sported red outfits, an homage to his Blood friends.

Soon public scrutiny led to a political backlash, one spurred, in part, by C. Delores Tucker, a black activist who spearheaded a fierce campaign against Death Row and its rappers.

"I love all the controversy. What we're doing is working. We're pushing buttons. Wait till the next record," Dre said at a 1993 American Music Association Awards ceremony.

Tucker's campaign was largely supported by then–Vice President Dan Quayle, presidential candidate Senator Bob Dole, activist William Bennett, and Senator Joe Lieberman, all of whom vocalized their opinion that gangster rap was detrimental to black communities.

As controversy surrounding Death Row continued, sales rose, and soon the politicians and activists directed their campaign toward Time-Warner, who still had a 50 percent stake in Interscope and had recently invested $120 million in Death Row, an investment on which they would most certainly see large returns.

"We African American women in particular are tired of being called hoes, bitches, and sluts by our children who are paid to do this by Time-Warner," Tucker said at 1993 televised news conference.

Bennett and Tucker frequented conventions, press conferences, and political events, asking for a ban on gangster rap. On the campaign trail, Dole often brought the issue up in his speeches. "A line has been crossed, not just of taste but of human dignity and decency," he said in one such speech, later mentioning Time-Warner by name.

They wanted Time-Warner to silence Death Row's controversial lyrics, bringing the fight from simple questions of decency to one of censorship. Soon, though, Tucker approached Michael Fuchs, the then-chairman of Time-Warner. She offered to head a new label, one that would celebrate "decent" rap that would be suitable for children. She asked that Death Row distribute its records through her label, making her the gatekeeper for gangster rap. She reportedly told Fuchs she could run the label with an initial investment of $80 million, money he would provide if she could get Knight to agree to the new deal.

According to legend, Fuchs then flew to Los Angeles and, along with Tucker, went to Dionne Warwick's house, where they were to meet Knight. They waited a rumored five hours for the music executive to show. He never did. Tucker now denies that she approached Fuchs to start a new label. Interscope filed suit against Time-Warner and Tucker upon hearing of their attempt to start a new distribution deal with Death Row. Time-Warner promptly sold its shares of Interscope back to the company.

"Whatever happens, we're going to stand up tall and be more success-ful," Knight said. "Only thing anyone making us do is be stronger and better" (*Welcome to Death Row*, 2001).

And the success continued. The label moved to the posh Can-Am Building in Tarzana, a small suburb 25 miles north of Los Angeles. Death Row also backed several other projects, including Death Row Films, Dog-gystyle Records, and Gotta Get Somewhere Records.

The Dogg Pound's album *Dogg Food*, released Halloween 1995, hit triple platinum.

TUPAC SIGNS TO THE LABEL

Named after an Incan revolutionary who led an uprising against Spain, Tupac Shakur was born amid a controversy that seemingly shaped his short life. His mother, Afeni, whose real name was Alice Faye Williams, claimed to be a member of the Black Panther Party, a 1960s black na-tionalist group. She delivered Tupac a month after being acquitted of 156 counts of conspiracy against the U.S. government. Afeni Shakur told her husband that Tupac wasn't his child. The future rapper never learned the true identity of his father. Afeni Shakur later narrowed paternity down to two men—a hustler known as Legs and another man named Billy Gar-land. Her husband promptly divorced her. With a son to raise, she took work as a paralegal.

As a child, Shakur often performed in plays, once having played Travis in *A Raisin in the Sun* with the famed 127th Street Ensemble in Harlem. He also went to the Baltimore School for the Arts, where he met ac-tress Jada Pinkett. There, Shakur played the role of the Mouse King in the Nutcracker. Then, Tupac's new stepfather, Mutulu Shakur, was found guilty of robbing a Brinks armored car, a robbery during which two police officers and a guard were killed. He was sentenced to 60 years, leaving Tupac, his half-sister, Sekyiwa, and his mother alone.

Afeni Shakur began seeing Legs again, but Legs was soon arrested for credit card fraud. Shakur moved her family to Baltimore, where a 15-year-old Tupac began writing lyrics and rapping while attending school. Milk-ing his New York roots, Shakur began calling himself MC New York after his mother took him out of the school, when a gang killed a neighborhood boy. She then sent Tupac and his sister to a Marin City, a small, diverse, poverty-stricken area just outside of San Francisco.

Shakur soon met Leila Steinberg, a white single mother who let him live in her house, and she took over as his manager. Using some connections, she spoke to Atron Gregory, the famed music executive who ran TNT

Records and managed Digital Underground. Gregory agreed to give Tupac a role as backup dancer for the popular act whose hit "Humpty Dance" placed them in the national spotlight. His "dance" included making sexual gestures toward a blow-up doll and demonstrating the Humpty Dance.

Shakur rapped on Underground 1991's *This Is an EP Release*, and he toured with the band through that year, recorded a demo, and sent it to then–Tommy Boy Records executive Monica Lynch.

But Tom Whalley, an A&R representative at Interscope, liked it and handed it to his boss, Ted Field, who let his teenage daughter hear it. The label soon signed Shakur. In 1991 his first album, *2Pacalypse Now*, sold 500,000 copies, prompting Time-Warner to increase their stake in Interscope. The top single off the album, "Brenda's Got a Baby," represents the album well: thoughtful songs that highlight social disparities that Shakur claimed to have seen around him. In "Brenda's Got a Baby," a cousin impregnates the 12-year-old Brenda. She initially hides the pregnancy, though her apathetic family soon realizes her secret. She eventually sells crack to feed both herself and her child, but after being robbed, she turns to prostitution.

Soon after the album was released, Shakur was involved in a gunfight with a rival group. A stray bullet—not from Shakur's gun—struck six-year-old Qa'id Walker-Teal, killing him. Though never criminally charged, Shakur later settled with the family in a wrongful death suit.

As his popularity as a rapper grew, he was able to pursue a movie career, landing a role opposite Janet Jackson in *Poetic Justice*. The actress insisted Shakur first be tested for HIV before a kissing scene.

In 1993 Shakur released *Strictly 4 My N.I.G.G.A.Z.*, which spawned two number 1 hits: "Keep Ya Head Up" and "I Get Around," both of which featured appearances by members of Digital Underground. Shakur soon moved to Atlanta. In October 1993, at the corner of Piedmont and North Avenue in the city's midtown area, he shot two off-duty police officers he felt were hassling a black motorist. The officers were later found to be drunk and in possession of contraband weapons they had stolen from the evidence room. Charges against Shakur were promptly dropped.

In December 1993, a woman performed oral sex on Shakur on the dance floor of a popular New York club. Later that night, they returned to his hotel room, where they had consensual sex. Two days later, she returned. Shakur claimed to have been sleeping and not aware she had arrived. She claimed he was awake and forced her into having sex with his friends. She immediately pressed charges.

Malik Lee, Snoop's bodyguard, recalled,

Three years before Pac joined Death Row, I met him in a New York hotel room while on the road with Snoop. 'Pac was standing by the window overlooking a crowded Manhattan street. A small crowd, including Kurupt, Daz and Snoop, surrounded him. This was before he was signed to Death Row. That night he began to rattle off his long list of court cases and their costs. Tupac complained that every time he tried to clear the slate, he was faced with new legal fees.

I remember how his passion, his desire to overcome his life's circumstances, took over the room. Everyone present stared into his excited eyes and nodded as Tupac concluded that jail seemed inevitable for him. Yet at the end of his hyped-up speech, he vowed to "make them pay," to rise above all his legal woes. (Lee, 1997, p. 157)

Less than a year later, his rape trial began.

"It's not a crime for me to be with anybody I want to be with," Shakur told a local broadcast station in a street interview on November 29, 1994. "But it is a crime for that girl to turn it into a rape charge. It was her who sodomized me. It wasn't me that went down to the dance club and ate her out. It was her who, at the dance floor, who had oral sex with me. She should be charged, not me."

Shortly after midnight the next night, Shakur was walking through the lobby of Quad Recording Studios in Manhattan to meet Biggie Smalls, Sean Combs, and Randy "Stretch" Walker when three men approached him, demanding money. At least one of the men then opened fire, shooting the rapper five times.

Even as medics loaded Shakur into the ambulance, he shot a defiant middle finger toward cameras. At Bellevue Hospital Center, he immediately underwent emergency surgery. A few hours later, barely awake from the anesthesia, Shakur checked himself out of the hospital. He wanted to attend the last day of his trial.

He was found guilty and was later sentenced to serve four and a half years at Clinton Correctional Facility in upstate New York. Once he was there, Smalls, Combs, and Interscope largely ignored him. Shakur rarely had visitors, save his longtime girlfriend Keisha Morris, whom he married while in jail, a marriage that was later annulled.

Suge Knight, though, began to visit Shakur. Nearly a year into his sentence, and in an agreement rumored to have been signed on toilet paper, Shakur joined Death Row with a promise to release three records. In exchange, Knight posted a $1.4 million dollar bail on a pending appeal of the conviction. Just as Eazy had gotten Dre out of jail, spurring their alliance in 1986, Knight had bailed Shakur out, requiring albums in return.

"Now … Tupac was living out every bad-boy rapper's dream: He was out on bail and riding shotgun with Suge Knight, the most feared man in the music business," Lee wrote (1997, p. 157).

Once out of jail and in Los Angeles, Shakur worked furiously, writing and recording his first song in less than an hour in the studio. He was soon armed with an arsenal of fierce songs unlike his earlier works. These songs were angrier, with lyrics that glorified what Death Row had come to stand for: cocky confrontational lyrics set to G-funk's relaxed grooves. There was none of Shakur's standard social commentary on this album; his soul-searching was replaced by a celebratory extolment of thug life. These songs went on to appear on his two-disc, 27-song album *All Eyez on Me*, an album that, after being released on February 13, 1996, eventually hit platinum nine times over. He recorded the album in less than two weeks. Many Death Row artists appeared on the discs, including Snoop, Daz, and Kurupt. Dre produced a few tracks on the album, though Johnny J. produced most of *All Eyez on Me*. By now, Dre was largely absent from the studio, a decision based largely on the atmosphere there.

"I read that there were differences, but I can't pinpoint what those differences were," former Death Row publicist George Pryce said (*Dr. Dre, Attitude Surgeon*, 2003). "I did know that Dre—that after several times, I never saw him at the office anymore. I'd have to go wherever he was to do my job when it concerned him, you know, for interviews and so on. I think that was because he was a creative person, [and] maybe he was distancing himself from that side of it so that he could totally concentrate on his creativity."

VIOLENCE AT DEATH ROW

Violence inside Death Row grew as steadily as the business's success. In the very beginning, back during the production of *The Chronic*, Snoop, Dre, and the rest of the label's roster often smoked marijuana, drank cheap malt liquor, and worked all hours of the night, keeping largely to themselves. Many of the original group held gang affiliations—for example, there was Knight's alignment with the Bloods, and Snoop was a well-known Crip. All was well, though, and many cited the label as a positive place for its ability to bring together members of such opposing gangs.

Knight ran Death Row like it was a gang, using violence or the threat of violence to get his way. But Knight wasn't a gangster. He had parents who were still together; he graduated high school and attended college.

It wasn't until his time with Death Row that Knight actively claimed a gang affiliation.

"The problem with individuals who come from the streets who are not truly entrenched in that world [is] they don't understand the rules, and they think that money puts them in a situation where they can control the rules and change the rules," said Michael Harris, the incarcerated felon who provided the initial funding for the label (*Welcome to Death Row*, 2001).

But as the label gained street credibility largely because of Knight's notoriety and Dre's fame, the Death Row entourage grew to include many new artists, almost all of whom kept a gang affiliation. Knight especially invited Bloods up to the studios. Many of the Death Row artists were aligned with gangs, and friends involved in these gangs would show up at the studio. Dre was one of the only ones on the Death Row roster without a well-known affiliation, a fact that may have helped along his professional attitude amid the violent atmosphere that began to foster. Soon, Knight, already well-known for his aggressive tendencies, led the pack in both threats and action.

During the making of *The Chronic*, one of the first such incidences pitted two brothers against Knight, who, angry about their challenging his authority over the use of a pay phone, retaliated with rage. Knight, who ran the studio as much as Dre did, felt he was the true boss at Death Row, being also responsible for most managerial tasks.

Knight stripped, pistol-whipped, and beat the two brothers—rapper Lynwood Stanley and his brother George Stanley—after Lynwood Stanley used a payphone reserved only for calls from Harris. The phone was restricted to calls only from Harris because he was in prison and could call only occasionally.

The Stanley brothers told Knight that they were Dre's guests and that he had said they could use the payphone. "By challenging Suge about the phone and also challenging Suge about his authority, they just found themselves in an awkward position," Harris said. Knight felt that the studio was his domain and that to allow someone to take a stand against him would lessen the respect others held for him.

Suge apparently left the studio, going down to his car to grab a gun. Once upstairs again, Suge fired at least one shot, and the bullet lodged in the wall behind the men.

The beating, which started in a break room, continued to the studio, where Knight ordered all the artists, including the D.O.C., upstairs to another room.

Knight used the gun to pistol-whip Lynwood Stanley. He then ordered the men to strip, forcing them to lie on the floor. In a move common in stereotypical gangster movies, Knight removed Lynwood Stanley's wallet, taking his identification card and claiming he would hunt him down if they went to the police. He then allowed the brothers to dress and leave. The artists who had gathered upstairs slowly made their way back to the studio, where blood had pooled on the floor.

The Stanley brothers did, however, go to the police, who quickly returned to the SOLAR building, looking for Knight. Someone downstairs quickly alerted everyone in the studios, where "everybody went crazy," said artist manager Lamont Bloomfield (Ro, 1998, p. 87). "Motherfuckers just ran! Like they were trying to get out a rock house knowing cops was on the way. People were screaming, leaving out the back, yelling, 'They coming up the elevator.'

"Others yelled, 'Take all the weapons out!' They were locking themselves in rooms—all kinds of shit. It was just a big ol' mess. Next thing you know, the police were rushing up … looking for people" (Ro, 1998, p. 87). The Stanley brothers quickly pointed out Knight, as well as a bullet burrowed in the wall. And true to a spoken Death Row code, nobody talked to the police, although Knight was promptly arrested. Later, in 1993, the Stanley brothers sued Knight, who settled the case for $1 million.

Knight also reportedly paid for members of the Bloods to accompany him on trips, acting as an entourage that occasionally reached about 50 men. These men often accompanied him on trips to Las Vegas and to local venues in Los Angeles and would frequently get into fights with opposing gang members and even with members of the Death Row roster. Knight also began more regularly appearing on magazine covers, most often dressed in his now-trademark red. He carpeted their offices at Interscope, having the red and black Death Row emblem blazoned into the center of the carpet. No one was allowed to step on it. The unofficial color of Death Row became red, much like the background of its logo, the color standing for the Bloods, the gang with which Knight now publicly claimed affiliation.

Stopping by the studio in early 1993, Knight became angry that his rappers were including Crips references in their songs, and Knight asked that artists—even those associated with the Crips—make favorable references to Bloods in their songs. For example, Knight's encouragement prompted Death Row artist Warren G. to note, in a rap on Snoop's *Doggystyle*, that he specifically drove a *red* 1964 Chevrolet. Warren and Knight often clashed over gang matters because the former claimed allegiance with the Crips, something that Knight did not like.

"The gang shit was something I had to deal with," said Death Row promoter Doug Young. "The left side of the room was all Bloods; the right side would be all Crips. You had to understand: that office was so fucked up when you first went up there. I don't think it was intentionally divided—Bloods or Crips. That's just the way it was" (Ro, 1998, p. 102).

Ex-convicts—such as an old friend of Knight's named Lip Dogg—largely served as security for the office. Young and many others have claimed that instead of settling beefs with artists, engineers, and others legally, Knight chose to handle matters with violence, most often in the form of a beating in a back closet used almost exclusively for violent purposes.

"You know how white folks like to do it—they like to scream at each other 'I'm going to get my lawyer on you!' But the new brothers wasn't doing it like that. They was coming through doors, coming through windows, and the whole nine on people," Young said (*Welcome to Death Row*, 2001).

One such incident in 1993 involved Simone Greene, a former staff photographer at Death Row. She described the incident in the documentary *Welcome to Death Row*:

> I wasn't the only lady that got beat up. Suge grabbed me by my feet and everything went haywire. This girl cold-cocked me, loosened up my teeth. I had two black eyes. David Kenner stood up and watched. Somebody else videotaped it, and I kicked Suge in his nuts and I got the hell up out of there. (*Welcome to Death Row*, 2001)

DRE BECOMES SCARCE AT DEATH ROW

Not long after *Doggystyle* was released in 1993, Dre was rarely in the office, choosing instead to spend his time in the studio, producing tracks for upcoming releases. Knight and Dre would meet periodically, but past that, they rarely crossed paths. As Knight became more involved with the Bloods, most notably the Tree Top Pirus, the band of Bloods from his childhood whose members were now his closest friends, his personality became even more violent.

"He wasn't all that violent until he got around his people. That's when he pulled the cape out from behind his suit and turned into Superman! These ol' penitentiary niggas he brought in were the ones I feared more than anybody. I knew they'd jump in front of a bullet for this man—'cause they never had nothing" (Ro, 1998, p. 118).

In 1994, Knight hired Daryl Henley, a former Rams player with no music industry experience, to act as general manager of the label. Soon after taking the job, Henley was arrested, convicted, and imprisoned for a cocaine trafficking ring he ran on the side. Knight often filled the office with old friends recently released from jail. Because of this, a prison mentality began to pervade the office, with people like Young claiming that working at Death Row soon became akin to working at a jail with each employee left on their own to defend themselves against any outbreak of violence.

Decisions like these were what led Dre to keep more to himself, interacting with Knight only when necessary. The change came slowly, over the course of two years, with his dissent from Death Row becoming more clear as Knight publicly became more "street," ultimately driving away Dre and former Death Row artists D.O.C. and RBX.

Of the original group of artists signed, RBX eventually ended up leaving Death Row first because of an ongoing "issue" with Knight that eventually erupted into a fight over some fried chicken. After a show at the Chicago's New Regal Theater in 1994, RBX, Snoop, and Tha Dogg Pound all went backstage, finding eight containers filled with chicken. Tired and hungry, RBX quickly ate the chicken, with the rest of the group soon following suit. Soon, though, Knight came into the dressing room and was instantly enraged upon seeing that the chicken was almost all gone. He had bought the food for his large entourage. He and RBX argued, and Knight pulled a gun. RBX quickly backed down. As soon as he returned home to Los Angeles, though, RBX told Dre he was quitting the label, claiming that the chicken fight was "one of many straws that broke the camel's back" (Ro, 1998, p. 120).

After a brief stint at Disney's Hollywood Basic, RBX went to Giant Records, recording an album called *AWOL: Escape from Death Row.* The album was quite critical of Dre and the label, with lyrics that prompted Snoop to stop talking to him. The album attracted scant media attention, though fans largely embraced the album because it allowed them to catch a glimpse inside the famed label without having ever stepped in its doors. Through his lyrics, RBX described the violence and attitude at the label in scathing rhymes.

The D.O.C. left soon after that, claiming that he was simply going to Atlanta to work with rapper MC Breed, another G-funk styled artist. "By the grace of God and good attorneys, they were able to leave," Snoop later said. "Everybody else was forced in a chokehold after that."

Sometimes, even those attending parties were forced to deal with Knight. Death Row hosted Dre's birthday party in February 1993 at the Strip Club in Century City. As strippers partied among industry folks and close friends, Dre celebrated not only his birthday, but also how sales of *The Chronic* had reached platinum. A huge marijuana leaf decorated a large cake as Death Row artists, supporters, and hangers-on stood around, drinking champagne and liquor. But at the party, Knight reportedly walked around with a huge silver serving tray, asking for donations to help pay for much of the liquor. Many said the request was less a question and more a demand of those celebrating.

By now, Dre was rarely in the office, instead focusing all his efforts on the musical aspects of Death Row, including his own videos. Dre chose to direct the video for "Let Me Ride," a single off *The Chronic*, in a shoot that included several early morning scenes in Los Angeles's Leimert Park, starring real Bloods and Crips drinking forty-ounces, as well as Muslims touting *The Final Call*, and white rap fans.

Once the music started, and Snoop and Dre had faced the camera to mouth raps, gang signs were thrown, making the video instantly unsuitable for MTV. Arguments erupted among the extras, between those in opposing gangs. Scenes were reshot several times before a clean take was finally achieved. Much like its stance on most profanity, MTV does not allow gang signs in their videos.

Other video shoots had similar results. At the shoot for "Gin and Juice" in late 1993, similar confrontations occurred. About the film shoot for "What's My Name," film crew member Johnny Simmons said, "Maybe it looked good on paper, but in reality it was a bad idea. 'Cause at eight-thirty in the morning we must have had about a thousand people: friends and enemies of Snoop Dogg standing out there in the crowd; people sucking on forty-ounce beers at the crack of dawn that morning. And tensions were really high. They were all going crazy. But that always happens on videos" (Ro, 1998, p. 117). Simmons recalled that many times at video shoots, he had to dodge beneath a truck because shooting erupted, most often at shoots for groups funded by small-town drug dealers. But filming for this video carried not only a larger budget, but bigger names as well, and would be on both BET and MTV if shot within certain specifications, such as no gang signs.

A small riot soon broke out, and audience members, crewmembers, Snoop, Knight, and Snoop's bodyguard were there. There were about three thousand in attendance, and the LAPD arrived with full riot gear. Knight drove through the crowd in a black Mercedes, stopping to pick up Dre and Snoop before leaving the scene. Simmons said he later asked police who was driving the car. He said the police responded in awe and respect that it was the owner of Death Row Records.

Despite the fact that he too was an owner of the label, after *The Chronic* and *Doggystyle*, Dre remained largely unattached to Death Row, except in production credit and video work. He no longer partied with the gang, nor did he spend much time at the office. Because of this detachment, Dre eventually easily walked away as if he were only an employee, instead of an owner.

Always noted for his professionalism in the studio, Dre seemed to wilt under these circumstances, his in-studio work coming along much more slowly than past albums, a fact publicly noted several times by both Knight and rapper Tupac Shakur. Both talked in interviews of Dre's absence, claiming it was his lack of love for the music instead of his decision to distance himself from Knight and the others.

Chapter 10

THE EMPIRE CRUMBLES

With increased success comes more money, and with more money comes, inevitably, more problems. And for a group of individuals famous for their aggressive style, gang affiliations, and an outspoken defiance, the problems can easily mount.

Although Dre first found fame in the late 1980s with N.W.A., his achievements at Death Row propelled him to an international stage not only because of his production and rap style and subsequent success, but also because of his unavoidable image constantly on MTV, BET, and popular magazines. Opposite of Knight, who played well as the iconic gangster, Dre increasingly found fault with the trappings of gangster rap and how the artists at Death Row began living the lives they projected in their music.

"It became, 'What kinda car does this person have. I gotta get a better car than that.' My house has to look better than that person's house," Dre said. "When the money started coming into play from Death Row, that's when the problems just went haywire."

MURDER WAS THE CASE

For Snoop, problems came in the form of a local gangbanger shot dead before he was able to shoot Snoop himself. Bodyguard Malik Lee unloaded his gun toward 20-year-old Philip Woldemariam, a member of a local Blood-affiliated gang that ran Snoop's neighborhood, the Los Angeles suburb of Palms, near the junction of the Santa Monica and San Diego freeways. Snoop, a Crip, lived in a small complex called the Vinton Palms simply because it was close to the studio.

Woldemariam, nicknamed Little Smooth, came to the United States at age six from Eritrea, a small African country nearly destroyed by war. Three gunshots wounds already pockmarked his slight frame, a testament to his time spent on the streets. Woldemariam was a longtime member of the Vinton Avenue By-Yerself Hustlers, and he apparently knew Snoop's gang affiliation. His fellow gang members claimed that Woldemariam was not one to back down from an argument, especially one in which he felt he was being disrespected.

And he'd sometimes go looking for a fight, defense attorneys alleged during Snoop's trial. According to them, Snoop, Lee, and their friends were simply minding their own business when Woldemariam and Death Row artist Sean Dogg got into an argument outside Snoop's apartment after Woldemariam accused them of throwing gang signs. Woldemariam, riding in the back of London's Chevrolet Cordova, argued with Sean Dogg through a rolled-down window. Some later said he was waving a gun, and Sean Dogg claimed that no one in their group was looking for a gang-related fight.

London, Woldemariam, and friend Dushaun Joseph left, headed toward Woodbine Park to eat some burritos they had bought earlier from a Mexican takeout stand.

Snoop, Lee, and a friend headed toward the studio in Snoop's Jeep Cherokee, doubling back when they realized they had left behind an important tape. On their way back, they saw the three men.

According to court testimony and an April 4, 1995, *Rolling Stone* article by Doug Wielenga, Lee said, "What's up?"

"I'm not trying to sweat ya'll, I'm just letting you know where you're at," Woldemariam replied.

Shawn Abrams, sitting in Snoop's backseat, rolled down his window, saying, "You ain't letting us know nothing, punk."

"Oh, so I'm a punk?" Woldemariam shot back.

Lee claims that Woldemariam reached for his gun. He pulled his first, firing off a full round. At least two bullets hit Woldemariam, one in his heart, the other in his rear. He collapsed, crawled to an adjacent alley, and bled to death.

Nine days later, on September 2, 1993, as Snoop was standing on the stage at the MTV Video Awards, appearing to promote *Doggystyle*, which would soon be released, police officers were waiting just outside, ready to arrest the rapper on a first-degree murder charge. But he already knew they were there. Someone had tipped him off a few minutes earlier. As soon as his on-air appearance was finished, he left out the back. A few hours later, both he and his bodyguard Malik Lee surrendered. Bail was set at an even $1 million. Knight put up the bond and asked longtime Death Row attorney David Kenner to represent Snoop. Lee remained in jail and, in a turn of fate, briefly shared a holding cell with Woldemariam's mentor, Monty Kalevich.

Their trial started two years later, on November 27, 1995. "This doesn't fit into the dream of stardom I had," Snoop told Wielenga in 1995 during the pretrial hearings. "It's messing with my mind, pulling me apart from my peoples. People think this shit is cool, that I like being notorious. It ain't none of that. This is nothing cool, nothing fun, nothing to laugh about. This is stressful" (Wielenga, 1995, p. 22).

Kenner, Snoop's attorney, said it was self-defense because Woldemariam reached for a weapon. Prosecution said Lee shot him as he was trying to flee.

"The D.A., he was a pain in the ass. He just tried to do everything in the world to make me seem like the most negative gang-bangiest criminal-minded motherfucker he could just imagine, and tried to paint a picture of me that just wasn't happening," Snoop later said in a televised interview. "It was just crazy knowing that's what his job was to do, was to get me locked up for life" (*Welcome to Death Row*, 2001).

They were acquitted of all charges on February 20, 1996. Convinced that Snoop was guilty, many outspoken rap opponents claimed his freedom came only because of the money Knight poured into Snoop's defense, though Knight maintained that it was Snoop's innocence that set him free.

"The problem isn't that Snoop was freed because we had money to get good attorneys," Knight told *Rolling Stone* reporter Doug Wielenga. "He was innocent. But lots of innocent people get convicted. Just check the letters from the penitentiary," adding that Death Row will "pick one or two cases a year where we think people are being unfairly prosecuted" (Wielenga, 1995, p. 23).

With his newfound freedom, Snoop realized not only that he was fortunate in his life, mostly with his career and with the birth of his son in 1995, but that he had lived his life in a negative way, not stepping up to the plate, that he had used this fortune in more negative ways, ways that resulted in the death of a man. Now with his acquittal, Snoop found a chance to change the course for his life, becoming a more positive role model to the legions of fans who followed him, as opposed to his previous role as a follower of the gangster style himself. He wanted to become a leader.

But as Snoop took on a more positive outlook, many at Death Row began to debase Dre, a movement spurred largely by comments Knight made about Dre's absence at Snoop's trial.

Dre never went to court with the rest of the Death Row entourage, something many at the label saw as treason. Knight claimed it was because Dre was too busy working on other projects, saying that Dre didn't feel it was necessary to show support for Snoop and, even more so, didn't want to show that support. Newly signed and still trying to impress Knight, Shakur was especially outspoken against Dre, claiming that although Dre was still one of his industry heroes, the fact that he did not attend any of Snoop's trial evidenced his apathy toward his fellow label mate.

But Dre felt he wasn't needed at the courtroom, a place he detests. He claimed that he hates the courtroom and that his presence there was unnecessary. Dre said that in the evenings, he and Snoop would often spend time together at his house and that Dre fully supported Snoop even though he did not attend the trial.

The trial marked one of the first public rifts between Dre and the rest of the label. It was around this time that Dre stopped coming into the studio as often, choosing instead to work at home. He felt that the atmosphere in the studio was not conducive to his work and that it was becoming nearly impossible to work around a constant entourage.

Knight often invited gang members to the studio, leaning toward a party atmosphere. The label's success brought on an atmosphere that shifted from one of work to one of play, with people in and out of the studio at all hours. Dre, always the professional, did not want to be in that sort of environment.

> Even other staffers found the environment to be difficult for conducting work, including George Pryce, former director of communications for the label: [The] atmosphere was a bit hectic. Off and on, there were all kinds of things going on, as there are in, I think, any record company in this day and time, and especially in any sort of hip-hop focused company. You know, people waiting, trying to get in with their music, a flurry of all kinds of things going on, and there were things I understand and [things] in the four years that I was there that went on behind closed doors that I know absolutely nothing about. (*Dr. Dre: Attitude Surgeon*, 2003)

Violence inside the studio continued, adding to the ever-present feeling of turmoil. But at the end of the day, it always came down to the money. Talks of new cars often replaced discourse on new rhymes. Shopping for jewelry often overshadowed production. Comparisons of houses, of women, and of clothes became the more common conversations.

But despite the more than $60 million in record and merchandise sales by 1994 and the additional funding from Interscope, Sony, and Time-Warner, Death Row often overdrew on its bank accounts. Accountant Steven Cantrock convinced a bank to let them overdraw, citing their large earnings as a promise that they would become current. But as cars and jewels were bought, limousines were kept on reserve, and Knight purchased a club in Las Vegas, the money seemed to go as quickly as it came. Cantrock was also later found to be embezzling money from the label, a fact that surely affected its bottom line.

Dre said the purpose of the label shifted from being a positive outlet for music to creating a living reenactment of old gangster flicks.

"In the beginning, it was all about niggers coming up, then it turned into a fucking Don Corleone thing. It was like a movie. You can come into his [Knight's] office but you can't step on the carpet's Death Row emblem and all that crazy shit," Dre told *Blaze* in a 1996 interview. "It didn't need to escalate like that.... I got tired of seeing engineers get their ass beat for rewinding a tape too far."

And as small battles regularly played themselves out in the studio, just down the road, Eazy-E lost the most important struggle of his life when his heart stopped, and doctors pronounced the icon dead.

EAZY-E DIES

On March 26, 1995, gangster rap pioneer Eazy-E died from AIDS-related pneumonia. He was 31. For more than a month, he had been at Cedars-Sinai Medical Center as an AIDS-related collapsed lung brought about heart problems.

Eazy was born Eric Wright in Compton September 7, 1963, to a postal worker and a schoolteacher. He dropped out of high school in the tenth grade, starting Ruthless Records soon after. Having achieved worldwide success with N.W.A., Eazy remained popular even after the group disbanded in 1991. His 1993 EP *It's On (Dr. Dre) 187Um Killa* hit *Billboard's* top 10. Eazy also hosted a program on an L.A. radio station, KKBT-FM. There were talks of an N.W.A. reunion, and upcoming albums, including another solo album, were in the works, as well as a double CD titled *Str8 Off tha Streetz of Muthaphukkin Compton, Vol. 1 and 2*. Eazy had already recorded 70 tracks.

All his life, he had had reoccurring bouts of bronchitis and a persistent cough. But that cough worsened, and when he could barely catch his breath, friends insisted he go to the hospital. Once there, doctors discovered the terminal disease. Eazy, ever outspoken, chose to publicly discuss his disease instead of hiding it under the guise of simple pneumonia.

Eazy first told the world he had AIDS through a statement read at a press conference held on a sidewalk just outside the hospital doors on Sunset Boulevard a few weeks before his death. His attorney, Ron Sweeney, read Eazy's words while family and friends—including new wife Tomika Wright, whom he had married just a few days before—stood by, crying.

With a strong, booming voice, Sweeney read aloud Eazy's statement:

> I may not seem like a guy that'd pick to preach a sermon, but I feel it's not time to testify because I do have folks that care about me hearing all kinds of stories about what's up ... fancy cars, gorgeous women, and good livin' ... Like the others before me, I would like to turn my own problem into something good that will reach out to all my homeboys and their kin, because I want save their asses before it's too late. I'm not looking to blame anyone except myself. I've learned in the past week that this thing is real, and it doesn't discriminate. It affects everyone. (http://www.eazy-e.com)

According to Sweeney, Eazy didn't know how he had contracted the disease, and the rapper didn't even know he was HIV-positive when admitted to the hospital. Quite promiscuous, Eazy had been sexually active since he was a preteen and had fathered at least seven children by six women. His wife Tomika and son Dominik, still an infant, had both tested negative for the disease, Sweeney said at the time.

After his statement, many of his friends, admirers, and even past enemies voiced their support for the man who had helped place West Coast rap on the map. His hospital room often filled with visiting rappers, including the Hammer (recently signed to Death Row), Dre, and Ice Cube. Snoop Dogg voiced his prayers by calling a L.A. radio station.

His illness and subsequent death were largely unexpected by the rap community and sparked some of the first urban HIV conversations. "It takes something like this to make the kids wake up, but it's terrible that it had to happen to [Eazy-E] because I got crazy respect for him as a businessman, an entrepreneur and a pioneer of the whole gangsta-rap genre," said Guru of Gang Star (http://www.eazy-e.com).

According to Dre, Eazy's open and honest letter about his disease brought attention to an epidemic many in the ghetto refused to recognize. "It's a real shame," Dre wrote in a statement released the day after Eazy's death. "I went to the hospital and saw him, but he was unconscious. He didn't even know I was in the room. It wasn't a pretty sight, man. It was sad" (http://www.eazy-e.com).

Eazy was one of the first rap personalities to emerge from the West Coast, his face having become synonymous with gangster rap. Through N.W.A.'s widespread publicity, other rappers across the nation were able to develop into caricatures of a genre that previously had been largely ignored by mainstream media.

THE EMERGENCE OF RAP BATTLES

Largely character-driven, hip-hop allows for distinct personalities to emerge much more than most other genres. Couple this with inherently violent themes, and hip-hop becomes a prime breeding ground for rivalries between labels or rappers.

One of the first known rap rivalries, or "beefs," surrounded the U.T.F.O. song "Roxanne, Roxanne," released in 1984. The song was the B-side of the group's single "Hanging Out," a cut that received little airplay. But "Roxanne, Roxanne" became incredibly popular in the New York area, as did U.T.F.O.

Shows across the city were booked, including one hosted by producer Marley Marl, disc jockey Mr. Magic, and Tyrone Williams, also known as Fly Ty. But when U.T.F.O. canceled, the three men became angry, a bitterness they loudly discussed outside a Queensbridge housing project.

According to legend, 14-year-old Lolita Gooden, a neighborhood girl, overheard the men and suggested they take their anger out in a record, with her playing the role of Roxanne Shante', the woman in the song "Roxanne, Roxanne."

The men agreed, and soon the song "Roxanne's Revenge" hit local airwaves. Using stolen beats from the original instrumental Roxanne song, the song was incredibly confrontational and amazingly successful, selling an estimated 250,000 albums in New York alone. U.T.F.O., along with their producers, R&B group Full Force, sued to have the song stopped. It was soon re-released with all obscenities removed and with new beats. U.T.F.O. decided to release a new version of "Roxanne, Roxanne," complete with a woman rapping the title role, answering to "Roxanne's Revenge." Radio stations would play the songs in trios, sparking even more versions of "Roxanne."

Soon, Sparky O's "Sparky's Turn (Roxanne, You're Through)" was released. Although it largely supported U.T.F.O., the group was said to be unhappy that yet another group recorded a Roxanne song.

Within months, more than 100 "answer" songs were recorded and released by a number of different acts, including Ralph Rolle's "Roxanne's a Man," a rap that claimed that Roxanne was a man who was sodomized while in prison and who became a woman when finally released.

The listening audience became bored with the Roxanne wars, turning to new "beefs" between artists, such as the ones between Doug E. Fresh and Salt-N-Pepa, as well as the "Yvette" war between LL Cool J and E-Vette Money, the first of such wars that LL Cool J would find himself in throughout his career.

As years wore on, similar rivalries emerged, including a long-running battle between Boogie Down Productions, featuring KRS-One, and Marley Marl's Juice Crew. Started in 1985, and continued in fits and starts, "The Bridge Wars" lasted until 2001.

The rivalry started when Queensbridge-based Marly Marl and MC Shan released a song touting their neighborhood as the birthplace of rap. KRS-One and Boogie Down Productions immediately retaliated with a song celebrating their South Bronx neighborhood as the real home of hip-hop. Soon the Juice Crew released a lyrical response, to which Boogie Down replied with "The Bridge," a rap based loosely on Billy Joel's "It's Still Rock and Roll To Me": "You're better off talkin' 'bout your whack Puma sneaker 'cause Bronx created hip-hop, Queens will only get dropped."

The feud continued for some time, though the release of "The Bridge" was arguably one of the battle's high points. Debates still continue as to who actually won the rivalry.

"You know, a lot of people be asking me that, 'Who really won that battle with the Juice Crew and Boogie Down Productions?'" said Juice Crew's Mister Cee in a recent interview with Jay Smooth of hiphopmusic. com. "I think about that a lot, especially when people ask me, and [there is] one thing that I do have to say. KRS One is an incredible rapper. He's a dope incredible rapper, but … what would his career be if he didn't make an answer record to 'The Bridge'?" (http://hiphopmusic.com). Though it was one of the longest-lasting feuds, Boogie Down and Juice Crew's war did end fairly amicably.

But few feuds have been as nasty as the one sparked when Ice Cube left N.W.A. in late 1989. After accusing Jerry Heller and Eazy-E of stealing money, Cube left for New York, where he worked with the Bomb Squad.

Once he was gone, the remaining members of N.W.A. insulted the rapper on their first two non-Cube albums, *100 Miles and Runnin'* and *Efil4zaggin*. Ice Cube didn't retaliate until his second solo album *Death Certificate*, in the song "Vaseline." But soon after the album was released, Dre and the D.O.C. left Ruthless, having discovered that Cube's allegations of unfair business practices were true: Heller and Eazy-E were, in fact, stealing.

Eazy then released the EP *It's On Dre*, which heavily criticized both Dre and Snoop. When with members of the press, he would show pictures of Dre in full makeup and shiny spandex, promotional pictures from his days in the World Class Wreckin' Cru.

A few years after the well-publicized beef between Eazy and Dre, and just after the rivalry between the East and West Coasts died alongside Tupac Shakur and Biggie Smalls, one of the most extensive rap battles came underway: the rivalry between Jay-Z and Nas. The rappers were similarly popular in New York, though back in 1996, Jay-Z had much more commercial success. In 1996, Nas refused to appear on Jay-Z's debut album *Reasonable Doubt*. The two remained friends, though, and Nas is even mentioned on the album's liner notes. But when Jay-Z released "This City Is Mine," a song seemingly claiming the empty hip-hop throne left behind by Biggie Smalls, Nas responded with "We Will Survive," a song that knocked Jay-Z off any throne.

The rivalry continued, coming to a head when Jay-Z made fun of Nas during a New York concert. Nas immediately responded, calling into a radio show and freestyling the lyrics "and bring it back up top, remove the fake king of New York," with other lyrics claiming that Jay-Z learned his rhyming style from Nas.

The pair appeared on record after record, each sparking another chapter in a rivalry that spanned several years. There were talks of a pay-per-view freestyle battles, plans that never were realized. Even so, though, mainstream media picked up the beef, sending even more listeners to the already-popular rappers.

The battle essentially broke down in 2002. In interviews, both rappers now liken the feud to a boxing match between two prizefighters. Jay-Z participated in at least four more rivalries, all of which have essentially ended.

Other rivalries have surfaced over the years, including a multi-song battle between rapper Benzino and Eminem. Benzino, who once published the hip-hop culture magazine *The Source*, largely used print to attack the white Eminem, who Benzino claimed was racist. This beef ended in court, with Benzino paying a large amount of money to Eminem for copyright infringement and defamation. Some advertisers, including Interscope and Elektra Records, stopped advertising in the magazine. Eminem lyrically linked up with hip-hop magazine *XXL*, sending Interscope advertising and artists to the smaller magazine.

EAST VERSUS WEST

Few battles have been as deadly as the one between the East Coast and the West Coast during Death Row's heyday. As mentioned briefly before, the battle not only likely resulted in the death of two rappers, but also brought rivalries to a more personal level than seen before.

Though N.W.A. was popular during its day, as Eazy faded into the background, another rivalry emerged, the East Coast–versus–West Coast feud that ultimately ended in the death of at least two men, Tupac Shakur and Biggie Smalls, in 1996 and 1997, respectively. The men, at first friends, became enemies after Shakur accused Smalls of having set him up to be shot. In a song released in 1995, Shakur claimed to have slept with Smalls's wife, Faith Evans. Soon after their verbal rivalry began, both were dead in murders some still claim were a marketing tool to keep interest in the East Coast–West Coast rivalry—and the subsequent interest in Death Row and Bad Boy—intact.

East Coast rap dominated the industry built on a style born in the streets of New York. Stylistically, the musical differences between the two geographic areas are as wide as the area between the two places. East Coast rap drew heavily from its roots, whereas the G-funk style of West Coast rap complemented its common themes of women, drugs, and murder.

But as Death Row, *The Chronic,* and now *Doggystyle* continued to push their way to the forefront of mainstream media, and international focus shifted to the left coast, New York artists saw their status—and marketability—as the only true rappers diminish. West Coast rap dominated the charts the same as it did the airwaves. Beginning in 1994, a rivalry began to emerge between the two coasts, resulting in a battle far stronger than any seen before.

Whereas Death Row led the way in West Coast rap, Bad Boy Entertainment and Sean "Puffy" Combs ruled the East Coast scene. Combs worked his way up from the bottom in the music industry, starting first with Uptown Records, working with artists Mary J. Blige, Father MC, and Heavy D, before being fired in 1993. Soon, though, Combs formed his own company: Bad Boy Entertainment.

Combs brought both popular East Coast rappers Craig Mack and Biggie Smalls immediately onto his new label. Combs tried unsuccessfully several times to recruit rapper Tupac Shakur. Even though Shakur refused, he did often work with Bad Boy artists, forming a particular friendship with rapper Biggie Smalls. After a few successful singles, Smalls' *Ready to Die* was released in September 1984, to fair commercial success.

But as Bad Boy's popularity—and roster—grew, so did animosity between the two coasts. In September 1995, one of Knight's closest friends, Jake Robeles, was gunned down at an after-party held after SoSoDef producer Jermaine Dupri's Atlanta birthday bash. Both Knight and Combs were at the Platinum House when an argument erupted. Robeles was shot and killed, and Knight reportedly turned to Combs, claiming he was responsible for the shooting. Combs vehemently denied his charges.

"I'm not a gansta, and I don't have no rivalry with no person in the industry whatsoever," Combs later said in a *Vibe* interview. "The whole shit is stupid, trying to make an East Coast/West Coast war. East Coast, West Coast, Death Row, Def Jam, or Uptown. I feel nothing but proud for anybody young and black and making money. [Some people] want us to be at each other, at war with each other. Acting like a bunch of ignorant niggas."

But the war was just starting. Almost as soon as he was shot, Shakur began to publicly accuse Combs and Smalls of setting him up to be shot, accusations for which he claimed to find proof in songs such as Smalls's "Who Shot Ya," released shortly after his November 1994 shooting.

Shakur, ever the instigator, recorded a duet in 1995 with Smalls's wife Faith Evans, a duet that spurred rumors of a romance between the two. When asked by a reporter as to truth, Shakur slyly responded, "I never kiss and tell," though he claimed several times to have slept with her. Smalls responded in print, saying that Shakur's claims of having bedded his wife were untrue and that for Shakur to say this was a disrespect to a woman who had little to do with the beef between the two rappers.

A year to the day after Shakur was shot, Randy "Stretch" Walker was killed in an execution-style shooting in Queens. Walker, a hip-hop producer, was present at Shakur's shooting and had worked with the rapper. The two had also been friends, though their relationship had deteriorated after Shakur's shooting.

At the 1995 Source Awards, which were held in New York, Knight brought the feud to the stage. "If you don't want the owner of your label on your album or in your video or on your tour, come sign with Death Row," Suge Knight famously said at the awards ceremony.

Later, in his own speech, Combs tried to settle any dispute through conciliatory words. "Contrary to what other people may feel, I would like to say that I am very proud of Dr. Dre, of Death Row and Suge Knight for their accomplishments, and all this East and West needs to stop."

As Snoop and Dre took the stage to perform a song, the audience booed them, with Snoops saying: "The East Coast ain't got no love for Dr. Dre and Snoop Dogg? ... Ya'll don't love us?" His voice was incredulous while holding too a tone of confrontation, and the crowd answered back with boos, some standing, their hands waving downward.

Other awards shows saw similar displays, including the 1996 MTV Awards, as well as that year's Soul Train Awards, held in L.A. There, Biggie Smalls and Shakur saw each other for the first time since the 1994 shooting at Quad Studios, when Shakur was shot five times, a shooting he had always claimed was a setup orchestrated by Smalls and Combs.

According to Ronin Ro, the scene played like one from a Western. A gun was drawn, and "both camps circled each other like prey" (Ro, 1998, p. 282) It was then, Ro writes, that Biggie realized that his former friend Shakur was no longer the man he had known before, having now taken to movie-like violence to solve problems. Despite this, their standoff ended without violence.

The rivalry continued, becoming more heated as Death Row announced the opening of an East Coast subsidiary called Death Row East. They announced the signing of former Bad Boy artist Craig Mack in several full-page ads that ran in several hip-hop magazines. Mack now claims he never signed to the label.

Magazines like *Source* heavily played up the rivalry, frequently featuring articles about both camps. "It was the media that blew it up, you know, you're seeing certain things that somebody said, highlighted in magazines about the West Coast and vice versa and it just boiled over from there," Dre said.

Soon, controversy, rather than talent and music, became one of Death Row's main commodities, though Mobb Deep did release "L.A., L.A.," an insult-filled response to Snoop's "New York, New York."

"There's enough room in this business for two young black males who are entrepreneurs to exist," said journalist Kevin Powell. "I mean, can you imagine if Al Bell and Jerry Gordon were fighting, if the Temptations had beef with the Four Tops. It sounds fucking retarded when you think about it."

Combs reportedly became increasingly tired of the feud, spurred along even more by the release of Shakur's "Hit Em Up," a scathing attack on the Bad Boy camp.

"I'm ready for (this beef) to come to a head, however it gotta go down," Combs said in a 1996 *Vibe* interview. "I'm ready for it to be out of my life and be over with. I mean that from the bottom of my heart. I just hope it can end quick and in a positive way, because it's gotten out of hand."

TUPAC KILLED

Perhaps tired from the constant arguing, Shakur began to step away from Death Row, planning to instead focus on the more positive aspects of his life. In the summer of 1996, Shakur was ready to make the change. With more than a hundred songs recorded for the last of his three-album obligation to Death Row, he would soon be free to talk to other companies, possibly Warner Brothers. He had two movies slated to soon hit theaters. He sent a letter to Kenner officially dismissing him as his attorney. Interested in further pursuing a career in movies, Shakur formed a company called Euphanasia to receive scripts. He and his girlfriend Kidada Jones talked of having children. He also talked about funding sports teams and a children's center in South Central L.A. (Ro, 1998, p. 291).

But despite his desire to leave the label, and knowing how Knight had reacted to both Dre's and Sam Sneed's departure, Shakur kept his plans largely to himself. He decided to join fellow Death Row label mates in Las Vegas on September 7, 1996, to attend the Mike Tyson–Bruce Sheldon fight at the MGM Grand. He had several misgivings about attending the fight, ones that he told Jones. She asked him to wear a bullet-resistant vest, but he claimed it was too hot. He left, unprotected.

The fight ended in a quick knockout, and the Death Row entourage left the fight and headed for the lobby. There, Shakur encountered Orlando "Baby Lane" Jones, a well-known Crip involved with stealing a Death Row gold chain earlier that year.

Knight, Shakur, and the rest of the Death Row entourage descended on Jones, kicking and pummeling him in a display caught on the MGM's gritty black and white security cameras. Satisfied with the beating, the group ran for the exit, and Shakur returned to his room at the Luxor.

He soon went to Knight's house, where the Death Row group piled into cars, heading for Knight's Club 662, where Run-DMC was performing. Knight and Shakur were leading the convoy in a black BMW, with Knight at the wheel. At least seven cars were following behind.

The convoy stopped at the intersection of East Flamingo Road and Koval Lane, just off the Vegas strip. A white Cadillac with California plates pulled beside the BMW, its driver's side window just a few inches from the passenger side where Shakur was sitting. A hand extended and in it, a gun. Shots were fired, at least 10, with glass shattering as fans standing on the sidewalk screamed. Shakur, desperate to escape the bullets, scrambled for the backseat, but it was too late. Bullets ripped into his body, two in his chest, directly through his "Thug Life" tattoo. A third bullet hit his leg, another his thigh. Glass sliced his head. Blood was everywhere. Shakur climbed to the backseat, where he lay, his chest heaving. Even with two tires flattened by bullets and the windshield shattered, Knight headed for the hospital, stopping only when realizing that police and an ambulance were behind him. They took both men to the hospital, though Knight only had minor scrapes. Once treated, though, Knight reportedly left without much word. But others—including Mike Tyson, actress Jasmine Guy, Tupac's mother, Afeni Shakur, and the Rev. Jesse Jackson—waited to hear if Shakur had survived the bullets.

He was alive. Despite a considerable loss of blood and the loss of a lung, doctors expected him to somewhat recover. Fans crowded the parking lot, holding prayer vigils as police watched for any outbreaks of gang-related violence, instead finding the group friendly and visibly distraught over Shakur's shooting.

Back at Death Row, publicist George Pryce worked extra hours handling the crisis as artist Nate Dogg finished recording his album *Christmas on Death Row*.

"We're fucked up," Dogg told Ro. "We need help bad. That's my feeling. We run around killing motherfuckers, shooting all them people that's our same color. We got to be fucked up. I think everybody just lost hope. Just, 'Fuck it. No matter what, we end up dead or in jail so I'm'a just go out here and act the fucking fool.' Only comment at this time I can say about anything is pray for Tupac. That's about it. The rest of it don't seem to make no sense right now" (Ro, 1998, p. 297)

But those prayers would find no answer. On September 13, 1996, just before 4 p.m., doctors pronounced Tupac Shakur dead from respiratory failure and cardiopulmonary arrest. He was 25.

Shakur's death spurred a gang battle in various parts of Los Angeles, a war that would ultimately end in tens of deaths as Bloods and Crips fought each other for no reason more than association.

Despite this, Suge Knight is often cited as the symbolic triggerman, a mogul who ordered the death of his hottest rapper simply because he wanted to leave Death Row behind. This theory has never been proven.

Knight also remains a top suspect for ordering the murder of another rapper, one whose death ultimately ended the battle between East and West.

BIGGIE SMALLS KILLED

Christopher Wallace, known both as Biggie Smalls and as the Notorious B.I.G., was raised in Brooklyn amid the extreme violence and gratuitous drug use that marked the city in the 1980s. As a teen, he turned to those same streets as a dealer himself. Eventually, he was arrested and sentenced to a short stay in prison. Like many would-be rappers who find themselves locked up, Smalls realized he had potential beyond peddling narcotics to addicts, and upon release, he set off on his rap career.

In 1994, Bad Boy Entertainment released *Ready to Die*, a deeply complex yet lyrically accessible album that propelled Smalls to become the king of New York rap. But his friendship with Tupac Shakur as well as his association with Sean "Puffy" Combs led to a career marked by the East Coast–West Coast dispute that, as many believe, eventually killed him.

Smalls chose different topics than many of the other rappers coming out of New York at the time. Instead of more socially conscious lyrics, he styled his words after the gangster rap formula that marked the West Coast, a manner that many say pitted him against Shakur after the friendship between the two soured.

As Bad Boy's premier artist, Smalls found himself the target of many of Death Row's lyrical aggressions, especially in Shakur's *All Eyez on Me* and later in "Hit Em Up," in which Shakur claims to have slept with Smalls's wife, Faith Evans.

Shakur and Smalls came face to face only once, at the 1996 MTV awards. Within a few weeks, Shakur was shot dead. Smalls was almost immediately blamed for the killing.

Six months after Shakur's death, Smalls was shot and killed after attending a *Vibe* party in Los Angeles. Knight, along with his friends the Mob Piru Bloods, a smaller clique of the larger Bloods gang, were blamed, though their involvement was never conclusively proved. Although the case remains unsolved, its investigation unearthed several police connections that ultimately led to what is considered the biggest police scandal in Los Angeles Police Department history.

THE RAMPART SCANDAL

Soon after inquiry into Smalls's death began, LAPD detectives made a startling discovery. LAPD Officer Kevin Gaines dated a woman named Sharitha Knight, Suge Knight's estranged wife.

"Just the mere fact that Gaines was associated with that company—to me, it was an organized crime group," said LAPD Detective Russ Poole in the PBS documentary *LAPD Blues*. He continued,

> Having experience and knowledge of Death Row and Blood gang members being involved in the drug trade, it warranted further investigation. Detectives discovered that Gaines was, as they say, "living large" for a guy on a policeman's salary. He had nine credit cards in his wallet and a bill for $952 at Monty's Steakhouse, a preferred Death Row hangout. Kevin Gaines was beginning to look like a bad apple.

Suge Knight and his entourage spent many evenings at Monty's, where they received special service a la *The Godfather.*

Gaines, along with fellow LAPD officer David Mack, acted as off-duty security for many of the rappers on Death Row's roster. Soon after discovery of the connection between the officers and Death Row, Mack was arrested for robbing a bank for approximately $722,000. He had worked with bank assistant manager Erolyn Romero to steal the money, a heist that had taken the bank five weeks to solve. Once arrested, Mack began to flaunt his Blood connections. While in jail, officers searched Mack's house.

Posters of Shakur hung on the walls throughout the garage, as other memorabilia sat on shelves and ledges. In the middle sat a dark Chevy Impala SS, a car strikingly similar to that seen at the time of Biggie's murder. Eyewitnesses at the time said that the same make and model car had driven beside Biggie's car, and passengers inside the car showered bullets on Biggie.

LAPD officers began investigating the widespread claims that it was Suge Knight who had ordered Biggie's death and that the Impala in Mack's garage was in fact the death mobile.

The connections led to more discoveries, including the role of Rafael Perez in serious crimes, such as narcotics smuggling and murder. But once in custody, Perez told authorities false stories that led to more than 100 criminal cases being overturned, sparking LAPD's biggest corruption scandal, now commonly called the Rampart Scandal, after Perez's beat, an area of L.A. called Rampart, which is largely known as the most densely packed, poor, and dangerous part of Los Angeles.

Many of the criminal cases overturned included gang members who, upon release, sued the city for millions. More than 70 officers were connected with the widespread corruption, though Perez's testimony is still largely questioned.

The atmosphere in L.A. and in the Death Row studios was more chaotic than ever before, with death rapidly becoming a part of daily life. Even though Dre's decision to leave Death Row had come before Shakur's death, the circumstances leading up to the rapper's early death largely contributed to Dre's departure.

DRE LEAVES DEATH ROW RECORDS

For Dre, a watershed came after a 1994 leisurely drive turned into a high-speed chase with LAPD officers. Dre, drunk, tried to avoid arrest, though he was finally apprehended, charged, and sentenced to 180 days in jail. Kenner helped convert the sentence from full-on incarceration to simply a stay at a Pasadena halfway house, which allowed Dre to work during the days, staying there only at nights.

"When I got sentenced, my mom told me that jail was going to turn out to be a blessing in disguise," Dre told *The Guardian* in a 1996 interview. "And she was right," he said:

> To be honest, prison was probably the best that could have happened to me in my life. Everything was happening so fast, the success I was having, all the money coming in, all the girls, all the partying. I never had a chance to say, "Yo, what do I want life to hold?" I had to find myself. And it was crazy. I saw a confused individual. A guy that wasn't sure what he really wanted out of life. It made me say "Yo, man, fuck those streets, fuck everything that's going on out there on those streets. Is this the life I wanna lead, or do I wanna be a businessman, be able to take care of my family, chill out, have fun and make money while I'm sleeping?"

Dre, a man who'd spent his childhood trying to escape the violence he saw on his home streets of Compton, had now become the icon of the role he had shunned earlier. While at Death Row, he became his image, morphing into the standard Hollywood persona he had grown up hating.

"You see, I got wrapped up in the Dr. Dre image, and all that old Hollywood bullshit," Dre said in another interview. "You know what I'm saying: the clothes, the jewelry, the fly cars with the big sound systems pulling up in front of the clubs. But incarceration brought me down to earth and actually turned Dr. Dre back into Andre Young" (Samuels, 1996).

This change in Dre spurred his newfound distaste for the brand of gangsta rap he had helped create. The label was moving in a direction Dre no longer liked, starting first with the signing of Shakur. The two never truly got along, though they were able to collaborate on what became a hit single: "California Love," a song originally meant as a duet between Ice Cube and Dre and released on its own, not appearing on any album until long after Shakur's death. The song was one of Dre's first steps away from gangster rap, instead carrying a triumphant party beat thumping beneath playful lyrics. But when Shakur stepped up the microphone, he cursed, evoking the standard confrontational style that marked most Death Row releases.

Shakur is also most often credited with the persistent rumors that Dre was gay, having said so several times publicly. He also openly criticized Dre's work ethic.

"He is a dope producer, but he ain't worked in years," Tupac said in a radio interview. "I'm out here on the streets ... whooping niggers' asses, starting wars and shit, putting it down, dropping albums, doing my shit, and this nigger's taking three years to do one song."

To Dre, Tupac's words were meaningless. "Tupac didn't know me, so what he was saying didn't affect me at all. He was speaking for someone else, jumping into something he didn't know anything about—which was his style," Dre told *Newsweek* reporter Allison Samuels (1996).

By now, though, Dre was finding it increasingly difficult to work in the Death Row studios. Even Snoop noticed the change in Dre and his reluctance to take part in most all Death Row activities.

Knight's entourage, which had expanded to include all sorts of people, often partied at Can-Am and also had expanded to include other producers, not including Dre. "There started to be tension in the camp among the other writers and producers," said Knight. "The folks who really did the production and wrote stuff on *The Chronic* and Snoop's first album started complaining about credit." Knight said that Daz actually produced more than half of *Doggystyle*. "But niggas was mad. Things wasn't right by them. I can't have that" (Ro, 1998, p. 266).

Knight also took credit for Dre's success. "But Dre didn't become Dre on his own," Knight said. "I went out and got the *Above the Rim* soundtrack for the company; we needed something. Dre didn't do nothing on it. He did one song on *Murder Was the Case*" (Ro, 1998, p. 266).

But the final straw came when Knight asked Dre to produce the album of Death Row's newest artist, Stanley Kirk Burrell, better known as MC Hammer. To Dre, Hammer was a has-been who had hawked KFC's pop chicken product once his "rap" album sales were no longer sufficient to support his extravagant lifestyle. He was not the sort of artist Dre wanted to produce.

"It was like being at a party and not knowing anyone there," Dre said in an interview at the time. "There was a lot of negative stuff going on there that had nothing to do with the music, and I wasn't comfortable with it. I was the co-owner and people—and I mean the wrong kind of people—were coming up to me on the street saying, 'I'm on your label.' I didn't even know them."

Dre decided to leave Death Row, calling Jimmy Iovine at Interscope to say, "I'm ready to bounce. Make me a deal, and I'll make you some hit records" (Ro, 1998, p. 269).

Interscope, eager to work with Dre without Knight, made a deal. Dre left Death Row, the company he had helped start just four years earlier.

"That was that," Dre said. "Very simple. I ain't got nothing to say to nobody. I'm just out. Period. I don't like it no more. The mentality there is you have to be mad at somebody in order for yourself to feel good or make a record. They have to be mad or say something negative about a certain person, instead of just laying back, getting off everybody's dick, making some strong music, and going on with your life" (Ro, 1998, p. 269).

Knight and Shakur spoke out openly against Dre, claiming that he couldn't handle the success and that he no longer had it in him to be what Death Row required.

"And what's [Tupac] talking about, Dre jumped ship?' Dre said in an interview with *The Source*. "Dre built the ship he's [Tupac's] on now. All that is bullshit."

Knight, true to his nature, focused mainly on the money. "Dre's departure wasn't a loss," Knight said. "I mean, if you have a multimillion dollar company with a billion dollars or so, and you own 100 percent and don't have a partner, then you don't have to give him nothing but his walking papers" (*Welcome to Death Row*, 2001).

But Knight did want Dre to give him the master tapes to several albums, including *The Chronic* and *Doggystyle*.

Knight—along with his usual gang of goons—showed up at Dre's house, first having someone call, claiming to be Jimmy Iovine, asking to be let in at the gates. At the time, Knight said that Dre called the police and that at least 10 patrol cars surrounded his home. A confrontation ensued, and finally, Dre released the tapes.

Dre, though, said there was no confrontation and said he was willing to hand over the tapes once he had made copies. While the carbons were burning, Dre said, Knight sat in Dre's living room, smoking a trademark cigar that he ashed on a coaster. Dre claims Knight talked of working together again, making more money releasing more albums. The meeting was amicable, Dre said.

They even met later that week, solidifying Dre's departure. An undisclosed amount of money exchanged hands, and Dre was released from Death Row.

Chapter 11

THE AFTERMATH

As soon as he knew he would leave Death Row, and plans for Aftermath Entertainment were underway, Dre finally found himself as his own man, no longer tethered to a manager, as with the World Class Wreckin' Cru's Alonzo Williams; or to a group, as with N.W.A.; or to a partner, like Suge Knight. For the first time in his career, Dre was alone and able to finally do exactly as he wanted both inside the studio and in the office.

With Interscope financially backing his new endeavor, Dre officially started Aftermath Entertainment in fall 1996. The wild, unpredictable, and violent days of Death Row behind him, Dre wanted to showcase a variety of hip-hop styles, not just gangsta rap. He began working with artists from across the coast and with a variety of styles.

Dre staffed his new office with women, a decision based largely on the chaos and violence surrounding Death Row. He claimed that women—and black women in particular—ran business far differently than men did, largely because of their straightforward manner and rock-solid work ethic. It also seemed a full departure from the work environment Dre had most recently left, one of gangsters and violence.

He soon celebrated his second anniversary with Nicole Threatt Young, an interior decorator he married in 1995. The two had settled into his Los Angeles home, enjoying a private life that often involved small parties with friends on weekends. Long gone were the days of clubs, bars, and parties, and in their place a quiet domesticality had developed.

If his life was vastly different on a personal level, it was even more so professionally. "First off, I want to be known as the producer's producer," Dre said in a 1996 *Time* magazine interview. "The cellos are real. I don't use samples. I may hear something I like on an old record that may inspire me, but I'd rather use musicians to re-create the sound or elaborate on it. I can control it better" (*Time*, Fall 1996, pp. 44–5).

Once again in control of his studio, Dre returned back to the work ethic that had made him a superstar. One *Time* reporter wrote, "Dre works in spurts. This week he's had three studio sessions of 19 hours or more. Last week he did a marathon 56-hour session. If he didn't go to the parking lot for the occasional car-stereo listening test, he'd have no idea whether it was night or day."

Dre often kept an entourage on hand to break the monotony of recording, though this group vastly differed from the crowd hanging around the Death Row studio. Instead of gang members, friendly security guards, old buddies of Dre, and other musicians all sought Dre's attention, often telling jokes to make him laugh. On break, he would eat dinner, often a clamshell full of fried chicken, the atmosphere relaxed, and the mood lighthearted. Many in the studio would drink Hennessy cognac, or smoke marijuana, although Dre rarely, if ever, now indulged in the substances he had hailed in *The Chronic*. He was all business, and once he had finished eating, he'd announce it was time to get back to work, and the room would clear. In short time this approach worked well. Dre's newest effort was ready to be released.

DRE PRESENTS THE AFTERMATH

Dr. Dre Presents … The Aftermath, released in 1996, was intended not only as a public notice that he was no longer part of Death Row, but also as an introduction to the artists he had recently signed to his own label. The first single, Dre's solo "Been There, Done That," gave listeners an audio departure from the gangster rap Dre was most popular for producing. At the time, he told a reporter that gangster had exhausted its welcome and that sales for such music would soon fall because those rappers were now simply repeating themselves.

Even the video signaled the symbolic split from his Compton roots. Dancing a "ghetto tango," Dre, along with sexy, sophisticated couples dressed in evening attire, dance the evening away in an upscale ballroom.

Even if you know nothing about the man, Dr. Dre's "Been There, Done That" is a video strange enough to freeze a channel-surfer's thumb: a Busby Berkeleyan ballroom-full of sleek couples in evening dress, all of them black, doing the tango in subtly infernal light, to violin music as eerily insistent as the soundtrack to a fever dream," Samuels wrote in *Newsweek* (1996).

Although the album eventually hit platinum, it in no way compared to the commercial success of his other releases. Critics were particularly hard on the album, as were his fans and peers.

> I was incarnated in federal prison, and we're watching MTV, BET, and we see this song called "Been There, Done That," and to me that was a like a total fucking disrespect slap in the face for the West Coast. He shitted on everybody like, "I've been there, I've done that; now I'm this and I'm that." What the fuck? That's what started you [and] now you're going to shit on everybody? ... Nobody was feeling that. (Dr. Dre: Attitude Surgeon, 2003)

The video was nominated in the "Best Rap Video" category at the MTV Video Awards, but did not win.

Faced with the backlash from this album, Dre shifted gears some, focusing on his artists instead of his own releases. He produced The Firm's Nas, Foxy Brown, AZ, and Nature Present the Firm: The Album, which released in 1997 to similar disappointing sales and reviews, though it too eventually reached platinum sales.

"I was hanging out with Mike [Tyson] one day, and he straight out said, 'Man, everybody's saying it's over for you. What you going to do.' ... The word on the street was I couldn't do it anymore," Dre said in a later Newsweek article. "One writer said my only prayer was to work with Snoop again" (Samuels, 2000).

In some ways, the writer was right. Though Dre would never work with Snoop the same way he did during the early days of Death Row, it was collaboration with the rapper that helped bring Dre, and the West Coast, back to hip-hop's center stage.

CHRONIC 2001

Released in November 1999, Dre's Chronic 2001 brought back to fans the sounds they'd lovingly become accustomed to, relaxed beats leaning more toward a party atmosphere than a self-righteous celebration of money and a disregard for roots, as many felt about "Been There, Done That."

The album represented a turning point for Dre in his production style, as well as in his choice of subject matter. It was a mature record that showed not only his growth as an experienced producer, but also his ability to transcend many topics, staying largely away from the age-old subjects of drugs and women. Instead, the album was more about the music, using more complex beats to support innovative stylistic themes. The album had two versions: one with lyrics and one without. *Chronic 2001* sold well in both formats.

Featuring Snoop, Xhibit, Hittman, Mary J. Blige, Kokane, Kurupt, and old friend MC Ren, *Chronic 2001* propelled Dre back to the top of the hip-hop scene. Although it didn't reach the sales of the original *Chronic*, many credit this album with firmly placing Dre back in the hip-hop world.

The album's first single, "Still D.R.E.," brought Snoop and Dre together again. The single—and subsequent video—proved to longtime fans, critics, and peers that Dre could still hold his own among hard-core rappers. The Dre that millions had followed before had returned.

"When Dr. Dre's *Chronic 2001* came out, [and] he came out with that video 'Still Dre Day,' we were like okay, that'd the Dr. Dre we know, from N.W.A., from Death Row, from Snoop Dogg, and when he came with that, it was like okay—he's back home with the low riders, and it was hot…. The love was back" (*Dr. Dre: Attitude Surgeon*, 2003).

The single "Still D.R.E." featured a lineup similar to that of *The Chronic*, with Snoop featuring heavily in the song, and with Nate Dogg involved as well. Dre chose the song as the best way to reintroduce himself to the public, playing largely on the single's energy and enthusiasm, which works well in a club setting, a fact that had helped propel *The Chronic* in 1992.

Even the video heralded back to the familiar beginning days of Death Row records, complete with a street party:

> I chose to do the video to "Still D.R.E." that way because a lot of people out in the streets were like, "Yo, when you going to get back to some of that 'Nuthin But a G Thang,' 'Let Me Ride' kinda joint." I was like, "Okay, well, let me try to hit 'em with this and just make it still look a little futuristic." So we had to take it back to the neighborhood, take it back to the cars, you know, the girls dancing, and everybody just having a real fun time. (Kenyatta, 2000, p. 53)

Dre said the creative vibe that had fueled *The Chronic* was alive and well with *Chronic 2001*. "It felt real good to get back with all the guys from the first *Chronic* album. When they came in the studio, it was just like we were never apart," Dre said in a televised interview with MTV in 1999. "It was a weird feeling, like, okay, everybody just came in and grabbed pens and papers and, you know, [started] doing [their] thang. It was just fun. Lots of laughter, and we had fun doing the songs" (Kenyatta, 2000, p. 54).

The album features a song called "The Message," a duet between Dre and Mary J. Blige mourning the death of his younger brother Tyrece Young, who had died years back in a gang fight. Originally, Dre did not want the song to appear on the record because it evidenced a certain vulnerability Dre had done well to hide throughout his career in the guise of a gangster. But in sharing that softer side, Dre almost instantly progressed from simply the creator and epitome of a certain style to an iconic and complex musician. Producing and rapping such a personal song would have never occurred to a younger Dre. But now, older and more experienced, Dre decided to put more of himself on record.

It was also in *Chronic 2001* that Dre introduced to the world his new protégé, Eminem, who was featured on the track "Forgot about Dre." "I wasn't worried that people would react against him because he's white," Dre once said in an interview. "The hardest thugs I know think this white boy's tight" (Kenyatta, 2000, p. 58).

Born Marshall Bruce Mathers III in 1972, Eminem rose from the trailer parks of Missouri and Michigan to the pivotal heights of being one of the best-selling rappers of all time, second only to Shakur. With a penchant for controversy, Eminem raps mainly of his hatred for his mother, Debra, and his ex-wife, Kim Mathers, often evoking terribly violent depictions of Kim Mathers's death.

Dre met the rapper by chance. He, along with most of L.A.'s hip-hop community, listened to the famous "Wake Up Show" on KPWR, Power 106 FM, which often featured freestyle battles between area rappers. Eminem battled on the popular show against Craig G. Juice, one of the more popular rappers in Los Angeles. Once the show began, though, anyone listening realized that Eminem outrivaled even the most formidable of rappers. He came in second to MC Juice in October 1997 at that year's Rap Olympics freestyle battle held on the show.

After that show was over, attorney Paul Rosenberg asked the host if Eminem could return, rapping on-air. He returned at least 10 more times. Rosenberg had already sent a tape into Aftermath, one that, by legend, Jimmy Iovine found on his garage floor. Dre decided to contact the men, asking them into the studio to talk about possibly working together.

Eminem and Rosenberg came to the studio, surprising everyone upon arrival. "[It was the] shock of a lifetime that he was a white guy," said Aftermath bass guitarist Mike Elizondo, who was there the first time Dre and Eminem met.

Regardless of race, Dre saw in Eminem something he needed: a talented rapper who shunned the traditional gangster mentality, instead using clever rhymes to address topics that ranged from domestic disputes to prescription drug abuse to poverty. Missing from his lyrics was the gangster mentality that had, so far, defined not only 1990s hip-hop, but also Dre's production style.

Eminem had already recorded *Infinite*, an independent album of which he had sold about 500 copies from the trunk of his car. No radio stations would play the album, most complaining that his style closely mimicked that of Nas.

But once he was signed to Interscope, and Dre began producing Eminem, his autobiographical lyrics on *The Slim Shady LP* took on a more playful tone, even when discussing more controversial topics such as disposing of his wife's body ("97 Bonnie and Clyde") or raping a young teen high on ecstasy in "Guilty Conscience," a popular song in which Dre plays the good guy encouraging a morally sound route.

The album sold more than nine million copies worldwide, becoming certified platinum four times over in the United States.

His next album, *The Marshall Mathers LP*, largely alternated between serious songs about his effect on his fans ("Stan") and more playful songs riddled with celebrity references ("The Real Slim Shady"). Like his songs on *The Slim Shady LP*, ones on *The Marshall Mathers LP* mainly sampled sound effects that accented his lines.

Receiving heavy media attention for Eminem's lyrics, the album sold more than 21 million copies worldwide, with the most sales coming in from the United States, where the album remained at the top of the *Billboard* charts for six weeks.

Subsequent releases—*The Eminem Show*, the *8 Mile Soundtrack*, *Encore*, and *Curtain Call: The Hits*—sold a combined 45 million albums. Dre produced the majority of the songs on these albums.

Dre appeared in Eminem's videos whenever he appeared in the song, most notably in the song "Without Me," off *The Eminem Show*. The video won four MTV Video Awards in 2002 for best male video, best rap video, best direction, and best video.

Eminem has received a total 39 industry awards, including an Oscar for the song "Lose Yourself" off the *8 Mile Soundtrack*. He is largely considered one of the greatest rappers in recent history, an accolade he owes, in large part, to Dre.

Since signing Eminem, Dre has worked with a number of top-selling rappers, including 50 Cent, whose 2003 single "In da Club" became an instant hit that is still continually played on the radio.

MENTORSHIP

After his mother was murdered during a drug deal, 50 Cent, whose real name is Curtis James Jackson III, was raised by his grandparents in the South Jamaica neighborhood of Queens, New York. A teenage street hustler, he went by the name Boo Boo until he eventually met Jam Master Jay of the famed Run-DMC, who signed 50 Cent to his label as a writer, not a performer. In 1997, Columbia Records brought 50 Cent onto their roster. His singles "How to Rob" and "Ghetto Qu'ran" singled out rappers and drug kingpins, causing his debut album *Power of the Dollar* to be instantly postponed. Shortly after being shot several times in 2000, 50 Cent left Columbia. Having heard some of 50 Cent's songs on a mixed tape, Eminem mentioned his interest in 50 Cent on MTV, and 50 Cent then contacted Aftermath. He immediately signed to a joint venture between Eminem's Shady Records and Aftermath Entertainment. Both entities are held by Interscope, which is 50 Cent's official label.

He first appeared on Eminem's 8 *Mile Soundtrack* in the song "Wankster," which gained widespread popularity. Under the guidance of Dre, 50 Cent then released *Get Rich or Die Tryin'*, which sold approximately 872,000 copies during the first week of its release.

In a setup similar to Eminem's Shady Records, Aftermath and Interscope helped 50 Cent establish G-Unit Records, which is a subsidiary of Interscope. In 2004, in a joint venture much like the one 50 Cent had signed just four years earlier, Aftermath and G-Unit signed Compton rapper The Game, whose debut January 2005 release, *The Documentary*, almost immediately hit number 1 on the *Billboard* charts. Dre, Eminem, Kanye West, and a few more artists produced the album. Eminem appears on the album.

The Game is famous for his feuds, including a long-running beef with Dre's former partner Suge Knight and the son of the late Eazy-E, Lil' Eazy-E. He also had many issues with 50 Cent, which ultimately resulted in his leaving G-Unit Records, ultimately forming his own such similar venture, Black Wall Street Records, which is held by Interscope and Aftermath.

Dre has also fostered Flipmode Records, run by rapper Busta Rhymes, who signed to Aftermath in 2004. While at J Records, Rhymes worked with Dre in 2001 on the single "Pass the Courvoisier," on his album *Genesis*. The rapper's style soon staled, though, and many fans claimed that collaborations with artists such as Mariah Carey had made him more mainstream than his previous work. He decided to leave J Records, immediately going to Aftermath. In a display aired by MTV in late 2005, a barber sheared Rhymes's trademark dreadlocks, locks he had never cut since age 17. He said the change was both a celebration of his work with Dre and Aftermath and a symbol of the change in his music, a style previously marked by versatility in lyrics and delivery.

In June 2006, Rhymes's *The Big Bang* debuted at number 1 on the *Billboard* charts, becoming his first number 1 album. Dre produced almost all of the album.

For the single "Legends of the Fall-Offs" off Busta Rhymes's *The Big Bang*, Dre transformed his studio into a cemetery to create sounds akin to a career dying.

"The song is about where you go after your career dies," Rhymes said in an interview with the World Entertainment News Network, continuing,

"Dre, when he made the track for the record, he tried to emulate this sound of a grave being dug and a coffin being put in this grave. He brought this barrel in the studio [and] he mic'd it up and he had dirt in it. The shovel going into the dirt symbolized the snare drum and the dirt being poured on the wooden coffin ... and these dramatic pianos was like the darkness of the beat. It made the song almost like an audio movie. Dre is crazy" (www.wenn.com).

There are still talks of an N.W.A. reunion that would prominently feature Ice Cube and Dre, although many industry insiders have said that those plans were canceled after Dre was unable to produce Cube's new album *Laugh Now, Cry Later*.

"Dre is like the Wizard of Oz—you follow the Yellow Brick Road, but you still might not get to him," Cube said in a June 2006 interview. "I've done more hit records without Dre than I have with Dre, but I'd love to work with him. Who wouldn't? He's the man. If he called me today, I'd be in the studio tomorrow" (www.wenn.com).

DRE'S LASTING IMPACT

It is almost impossible to listen to a modern hip-hop song that does not bear Dre's influence. With innovations in style that started with N.W.A., Dre continues to lead the pack in production. His protégés—Snoop and Eminem—are both considered among the top rappers to have emerged since rap was born on the streets of New York three decades ago. Dre has inspired and influenced legions of young men and women to chase their dreams, despite color or upbringing. As a man who rose from the streets of one of the country's poorest and toughest cities, Dre is truly the American Dream realized.

He is respected across the world, his influence reaching far beyond the U.S. borders. "What he did with his music was very influential for us because he created music that described the place of his origin, which is something we try to do," said Pepe Mogt, the composer who created Tijuana's Norten Collective of DJs. "Also his sound is just incredible" (*Time*, Fall 1996, pp. 44–5).

To fans, he is undeniably a hero. "He is the godfather of hip-hop," said Joey Lay, an aspiring producer in Atlanta who goes by the name

DJ Kool-Whip, in an interview for this book. "He's who made it [hip-hop] what it is today; he's who makes it so people like me might even have a chance. And even if I don't make it, if any of us don't make it, at least we tried, something I never would've done without having heard N.W.A. and *The Chronic*."

Snoop once expressed similar sentiments, having that said that Dre, through his success with N.W.A., inspired many in Compton to at least try. "He's [the one] who made us think we could do it," Snoop said in *Welcome to Death Row*.

To other producers, he is an icon. "Do hip-hop producers hold Dr. Dre in high esteem? It's like asking a Christian if he believes Christ died for his sins," wrote Kanye West in an April 2005 *Rolling Stone* article. "He's the definition of a true talent. Dre feels like God placed him hear to make music, and no matter what forces are aligned against him, he always ends up on the mountaintop" (West, 2005).

And that talent, which drives him to rage against the forces that would possibly hold him down, is what makes Dre easily one of hip-hop's greatest aspects. As Bushwick Bill rapped at the end of *The Chronic*'s "Stranded on Death Row," there are people in the world who don't know what happened, people who wonder what happened, and people like Dre and Bill, who make things happen.

Through his many albums, Dre has made it happen, creating an entire genre of music from scratch, propelling unknown rappers to super stardom, inspiring innumerable fans to chase their dreams, and asking the American public to recognize the problems inherent in black communities. Dre gave a voice to those previously ignored, and that voice has proven to be strong and enduring, inspiring public discourse and instilling a sense of empowerment, one that will surely persevere long after he stops producing.

BIBLIOGRAPHY

Chang, Jeff. *Can't Stop, Won't Stop: A History of the Hip-Hop Generation*. New York: St. Martin's Press, 2005.

Cross, Brian. *It's Not about a Salary . . . Rap, Race and Resistance in Los Angeles.* New York: Verso, 1993.

Death Row Uncut. Executive produced by Marion "Suge" Knight. Los Angeles, CA: Ventura Distribution, 2000.

DeCurtis, Anthony. "Music's Mean Season." *Rolling Stone*, 14 December 1989.

Dr. Dre: Attitude Surgeon. New Zealand: Leftfield Media Group and Chrome Dreams, 2003.

Gold, Jonathan. "Day of the Dre." *Rolling Stone*, 30 September 1993.

Gold, Jonathan. "Dr. Dre's Expanding Sphere of Influence." *Los Angeles Times*, 7 July 1990: section F.

Hendler, Herb. *Year by Year in the Rock Era*. Westport, CT: Greenwood Press, 1983.

Hochman, Steve. "N.W.A. Cops an Attitude." *Rolling Stone*, 29 June 1989.

Hunt, Dennis. "Dr. Dre Joins an Illustrious Pack." *Los Angeles Times Calendar*, 22 October 1989: 76.

Kenyatta, Kelly. "You Forgot about Dre: The Unauthorized Biography of Dr. Dre and Eminem." Los Angeles, CA: Busta Books, 2000.

Lee, McKinley "Malik," Jr. *Chosen by Fate: My Life Inside Death Row Records*. West Hollywood, CA: Dove Books, 1997.

Light, Alan. "Beating Up the Charts." *Rolling Stone*, 8 August 1991.

Light, Alan (ed.). *The Vibe History of Hip Hop*. New York: Three Rivers Press, 1999.

McDermott, Terry. "Parental Advisory: Explicit Lyrics: No One Was Ready for N.W.A.'s 'Straight Outta Compton.' But It Sold 3 Million Records and

Transformed the Music Industry." *Los Angeles Times Magazine*, 14 April 2002.

Quinn, Eithne. *Nuthin' but a "G" Thang: The Culture and Commerce of Gangsta Rap*. New York: Columbia University Press, 2005.

Ro, Ronin. *Have Gun, Will Travel: The Spectacular Rise and Fall of Death Row Records*. New York: Bantam Doubleday, 1998.

Sager, Mike. "The World According to Amerikka's Most-Wanted Rapper." *Rolling Stone*, 4 October 1990.

Samuels, Allison. "The Doctor Is in the House." *Newsweek*, 3 July 2000.

Samuels, Allison. "Last Tango in Compton." *Newsweek*, 25 November 1996.

Samuels, Allison. "Part Business, All Music." *Newsweek*, 18 December 1995.

Tyrangiel, Josh. "In the Doctor's House." *Time*, Fall 2001.

Welcome to Death Row. Directed by Leigh Savidge. Santa Monica, CA: Xenon Pictures and KDA Productions, in association with Oliver Entertainment, 2001.

West, Kanye. "Dr. Dre (The Immortals)." *Rolling Stone*, 21 April 2005.

Wielenga, Doug. "Rock and Roll: The Dogg Walks." *Rolling Stone*, 4 April 1995.

ADDITIONAL READING, REVIEWS, AND CRITICISMS

Banjoko, Adisa. "Dre Day: Damn, It Feels Good to Be a Dre." *Vibe*, February 2000: 62–63.

Bozza, Anthony. "Eminem Blows Up." *Rolling Stone*, 29 April 1999: 42–47, 72.

Bozza, Anthony. "People of the Year: Dr. Dre." *Rolling Stone*, 14 December 2000: 82.

Bozza, Anthony. "Q&A: Dr. Dre." *Rolling Stone*, 9 December 1999: 32.

Callahan-Bever, Noah. "Dr. Dre: Master at Work." *Vibe*, January 2005: 20.

Frere-Jones, Sasha. "Pop Music: Fifth Grade—Eminem's Growing Pains." *The New Yorker*, 6 December 2004: 119–21.

Goetz, Thomas, et al. "How Ronald Reagan Created Gangsta Rap." *The Village Voice*, 8 October 1996: 40–41.

Kulkarni, Neil. "Dr Dre: Ten Reasons Not to Forget about Dre." *Melody Maker*, 15 November 2000: 30.

Marcovitz, Hal, et al. *Dr. Dre*. Broomhall, PA: Mason Crest, 2006.

Pareles, Jon. "Can Rap Move Beyond Gangstas?" *The New York Times*, 28 July 1996: sect. 2, p. 30.

Ro, Ronin. "Escape from Death Row." *Vibe*, October 1996: 74–78.

Strange, Adario. "Angel of Death." *The Source*, December 1996: 102–110.

Strauss, Neil. "All Eyez on Game." *Rolling Stone*, 10 March 2005.

Strauss, Neil. "The Pop Life: Failure's Hard but Success Can Be Worse." *The New York Times*, 21 July 1998: E1, E5.

Whitehead, Colson. "Wild Wild West." *The Village Voice*, 24 December 1996.

Williams, Frank. "Let Me Ride: A Year in the Life of Dr. Dre." *The Source*, January 1997.

Williams, Frank. "Life After Death." *The Source*, July 1996.

WEB SITES

The official Web site of Dr. Dre: http://www.dre2001.com

A fan-based Web site dedicated to news and information about Dr. Dre: http://www.dr-dre.com

The official Web site of Dr. Dre's Aftermath Entertainment group: http://aftermath-entertainment.com

The official Web site of Dr. Dre's Aftermath Records label: http://aftermathmusic.com

A fan-based Web site featuring interviews, photographs, and a biography of Dr. Dre: http://www.drdre.us

Dr. Dre's online profile on the popular networking site: http://myspace.com/drdre

A collection of interviews, photographs, and articles about Dr. Dre: http://rollingstone.com/artists/drdre

INDEX

About the Authors

JOHN BORGMEYER is a former news editor at the *C-VILLE Weekly*, an alternative newsweekly in Charlottesville, Virginia. He was a contributing writer to *The Greenwood Encyclopedia of Rock History* (2005). He lives in Missouri.

HOLLY LANG is a freelance writer and editor. She has worked as a reporter for the *Birmingham Post-Herald* and the Associated Press.